Tony Augarde has helped to compile many English dictionaries for the Oxford University Press. He has written three books about word games, and writes a regular article about words for *Oxfordshire Limited Edition* magazine. He sets a weekly internet quiz for Credo Reference, and in his spare time plays the drums.

WORDPLAY

The weird and wonderful world of words

Tony Augarde

JON CARPENTER

Our books may be ordered from bookshops or (post free) from
Jon Carpenter Publishing, Alder House, Market Street, Charlbury, OX7 3PH
01608 819117

e-mail: orders@joncarpenter.co.uk

To place a credit card order please phone 01689 870437 or 01608 819117

First published in 2011 by
Jon Carpenter Publishing
Alder House, Market Street, Charlbury, Oxfordshire OX7 3PH

ISBN 978 1 906067 10 6

Printed in England by CPI Antony Rowe, Chippenham

Contents

Introduction

1   ORIGINS   9
Derivations
Borrowings
Eponyms

2   DICTIONARIES   17
Compiling
Word frequency
Swallowing the dictionary
Spurious words

3   PUNCTUATION AND GRAMMAR   25
Hyphens
Colonic irrritation
Parts of speech

4   SPELLING   32
A bad spell
Spelling reform
Spelling bees
Artificial languages
Text messages

5   FOREIGN PARTS   42
Idiotic idioms
Phrase books
Getting by and getting off
India
Americanisms

6   WORDPLAY

6   **NEW WORDS FOR OLD**   52
       Language change
       Coinages
       Needed words
       Words of the year
       Back-formations

7   **PHRASES**   67
       Clichés
       Idioms
       Allusions
       Proverbs
       Rhetoric
       Mixed metaphors
       Oxymorons

8   **PUNS**   80
       Daft definitions
       Punning names
       Punning headlines
       Advertising puns
       Double entendres

9   **SLANG**   89
       Slinging words around
       Jargon
       Rhyming slang
       Pig Latin and backslang
       Blason populaire

10   **NAMES**   99
       Nicknames
       Pseudonyms
       Real names
       Pet names
       Naming horses
       Car names
       House names

11 VERSE AND WORSE   113
Nonsense
Nonsense words
Limericks
Double dactyls
Clerihews

12 LETTERS ALONE   126
Vowels and consonants
Phonetic alphabet
Keyboard words
Acronyms
Palindromes

13 ODDITIES   136
Contronyms
Unpaired negatives
Collective nouns
Outlandish words
Famous last words

14 **ANSWERS TO QUIZZES**   145

Introduction

Most of us use words so much in speaking and writing that we may take them for granted. Yet they can be fascinating. My involvement with words became "professional" when I got a job writing dictionaries for the Oxford University Press. I assisted with the four-volume *Oxford English Dictionary Supplement* (which updated the massive *Oxford English Dictionary*), helped to revise the *Pocket Oxford Dictionary* and *Oxford School Dictionary*, and I was Editor of the *Oxford Intermediate Dictionary* and *Oxford Dictionary of Modern Quotations*. I also wrote three books about word games, which led to my being employed to write a regular "Wordplay" article for *Oxfordshire Limited Edition*, the monthly colour magazine of *The Oxford Times*.

Having written these Wordplay articles for more than ten years, it seemed a good idea to collect some of them into the more permanent form of a book, which is what you are holding now. Most of the articles have been revised and updated. The result is (I hope) an informative book about the English language, and particularly its more entertaining aspects.

The English language is one of the most important things the British have – and its value is underlined by its widespread use throughout the world. And language is possibly the one thing which distinguishes humans from other animals. As Maya Angelou wrote: "Language is man's way of communicating with his fellow man and it is language alone which separates him from the lower animals".

Because it is so important, language often causes controversy. Yet it can also be used playfully – to create innumerable games and forms of wordplay.

Join me in looking at some of the serious (and not-so-serious) aspects of words and the ways we use them – or misuse them. And try to solve the quizzes which are dotted around the book.

I am very grateful to Tim Metcalfe, Editor of *Oxfordshire Limited Edition*, for giving his blessing to this project. And my thanks also go to the publisher, Jon Carpenter, for letting this book see the light of day.

Tony Augarde

1

Origins

Derivations

A programme on British television called *What's in a Word?* featured a presenter who purported to tell us the origin of words and phrases. For example, he might wander around an ancient kitchen, explaining that "sauce" originally meant a salted vegetable, which was served on a "saucer". He might go on to tell us that "to give someone the cold shoulder" derives from the habit of serving hot meat to a welcome visitor but giving only a cold shoulder of mutton to someone who is unwelcome or who has outstayed his welcome.

It was interesting stuff, although some of his derivations were disputable. For example, he asserted that the phrase "you'll have to whistle for it" comes from a whistle attached to tankards so that drinkers could call for another drink. This seems unlikely, as the phrase "whistle for it" implies that you are unsuccessful in getting what you want. Equally dubiously, he told us that the common name "Pig and Whistle" for a public house comes from *pig* (a measure of ale) and *whistle* (= wassail). But Robert Hendrickson's *Dictionary of Word and Phrase Origins* says that the phrase is a corruption of the Norse *Piga Waes Hail*, meaning "Hail to the Virgin".

The investigation of word origins is called "etymology", which itself comes from the Greek *etumos* meaning "true". However, you can't believe every etymology you read – even those found in authoritative dictionaries. People so often cling to mistaken beliefs about the origins of words that lexicographers have a name for the tendency: folk etymology.

For instance, the word *posh* is often asserted to come from the initial letters of "Port Out, Starboard Home", referring to the supposedly preferred choice of shady cabins for those sailing from Britain to India and back again. Yet there is no firm evidence for this belief, and the word is more likely to be a corruption of some other word like *polished, pot* or even *tosh*.

Again, if you call toasted cheese-on-toast a *Welsh rabbit*, someone is bound to tell you it should be *Welsh rarebit*. Yet *Welsh rabbit* is the original phrase, derived from the notion that poor Welsh people regarded cheese-on-toast as the equivalent of rabbit. This is typical of the superior attitude with which the English have long regarded the Welsh. Hendrickson says that similar mockingly demeaning phrases were *Welsh comb* for the fingers and *Welsh carpet* for a painted floor! Indeed, the word *Welsh* originally meant "foreigners".

Another perennial question concerns the origin of *OK*, which can with fair confidence be traced to the American use of "OK" as a jokey abbreviation for "orl korrect", which was taken up by Martin Van Buren as an election slogan in 1840, since his nickname was "Old Kinderhook" (he was born at Kinderhook, in New York State). Some writers suggest that *OK* is connected with the Scottish "och aye" but I am unconvinced.

Other frequent questions include why we call sausages *bangers* (because they explode when grilled or fried without being pierced beforehand); why some people call ketchup *catsup* (they are just different ways of spelling a condiment that originally came from the Far East); and why *soap operas* are so called (they were originally dramas on American radio, sponsored by soap companies).

Nonetheless, if you treat it with care, etymology can be fascinating and educative. For example, it puts some words into context if you know that they derive from the names of particular places. Thus copper was originally exported from Cyprus; currants came from Corinth; denim originated in the French town of Nimes; and damask comes from Damascus – as do damsons.

Many people know that *goodbye* is a contraction of "God be with you"; that the *navvies* who built the early railways and canals were originally "navigators"; and that *October* and *November* come from Latin words for eight and nine because they were respectively the eighth and ninth month in the Roman calendar. But did you realize that a butler was someone in charge of the bottles? That grocers were once wholesalers, who sold only large (gross) amounts? That the jewel called an amethyst comes from a word meaning "not intoxicated", because the gem was thought to be a charm against drunkenness? And that a Xerox machine is named from the Greek word for "dry" because it makes dry copies?

Quiz 1

Identify these words from the clues to their origin.
1. Which cloth protects chairs from greasy hair oil?

2. Which fruity pudding gets its name from a German word for "whirlpool"?

3. Which indiscriminate weapon started life as a Dutch thunder-tube?

4. Which painting is made on fresh plaster?

5. Which game was named from a French hooked stick?

6. Would you put this sour wine on fish and chips?

7. Brides assemble this small bundle or truss.

8. Which game is a French railway?

9. These criminals got their name from an Italian word for "bragging".

10. This game is named from a Tibetan word for "ball".

Borrowings

Where did the English language come from? To over-simplify, we might say that our language originated as Anglo-Saxon (or Old English) – basically a Germanic language. It was influenced by Viking invaders, who spoke Norse – another Germanic language – and was also affected by Latin and French. The language changed further with such things as the invention of printing, the Great Vowel Shift (don't ask), Shakespeare's innovations, and the Authorized Version of the Bible.

You could say that this left us with the basis of modern English as we have it today. Yet our language continued to grow, particularly by borrowing expressions from other languages. These are generally called loanwords or borrowings, although they are not so much borrowed as taken without asking permission. *Loanword* itself is a sort of borrowed word – adapted from German *Lehnwort*.

In the Middle Ages, English "borrowed" extensively from French – primarily because French was the main language of the ruling classes after the Norman Conquest. This gave us terms like *attorney, bailiff, baron, court, duchess, duke, government, judge, jury, noble, prison* and *tax*.

Many French words came ultimately from Latin, another language which affected us after the Romans invaded. When England was converted to Christianity, we adopted such Latin words as *creed, martyr, mass* and *psalm*.

We borrowed more words from Latin during the Renaissance – like *carbuncle, malefactor, meditate, obvious, seraphim* and *testament* – which tended to be longer than the simple Anglo-Saxon ones.

Since then, borrowing has continued and even accelerated. Britain has taken many terms from France (probably because it is our nearest neighbour), including *beauty, café, chic, forest, garage, garden, niche* and *poison*. These words are not usually italicized because they have been fully assimilated into

English. Yet we often italicize such terms as *avant-garde, joie de vivre, risqué* and *savoir faire* because they still have a French flavour.

Attending a party recently, I wondered where the word *canapé* came from. Obviously it is French, but how did it come to mean a tiny snack on a piece of toast, bread or biscuit? And why does the *OED* say that it also means a couch? *Canapé* is from the same root as *canopy*, which comes from the Greek word *konops* meaning a mosquito. A canopy was originally a mosquito net but it could also mean a couch or bed covered with mosquito nets or curtains, and hence came to mean a curtain or covering.

The "couch" sense was prominent in France but *canapé* was used in Britain as a kind of metaphor to describe a small base with a covering (or "canopy") of food. A similar snack is called in French an *amuse-bouche* or an *amuse-gueule*, meaning something that amuses the mouth or gullet!

Another word that we took from French is *cravat*. Mercenaries from Croatia were employed by France in the Thirty Years' War (1618-48) and they had a habit of wearing neck-scarves. These appealed to the fashion-conscious French, who started wearing them and called them *cravates* – the French word for Croats.

The word *bastard* comes from Old French *bast*, which meant a pack-saddle. These saddles were often used by muleteers as beds when they stayed at an inn or slept in the open air: hence a *fils de bast* was an illegitimate child.

The borrowing was not only one-way. We took the word *beef* from the French *boeuf*, but the French stole our *beefsteak* and turned it into *bifteck*. France also borrowed our *riding-coat* but turned it into *redingote*, which we later borrowed back.

We also adopted vocabulary extensively from our other European neighbours: *coleslaw, poppycock, skipper, sloop, yacht* (and many other nautical terms) from the Dutch; *alligator, barbecue, cannibal, guitar, hurricane, macho, mosquito, sherry* and *siesta* from Spanish; *marmalade* and *molasses* from Portugal; and *bordello, broccoli, fresco, graffiti, opera, prima donna, stanza* and *violin* from Italy.

Italy has given us lots of valuable words. Because Italy nurtured some influential composers and set the standard for much of European music, many musical terms are in Italian, like *adagio* (=at ease), *allegro, contralto, libretto* (=little book), *presto* and *con moto*.

Where would we be without Italian *ditto* (literally meaning "said" or "aforesaid" – from Latin *dictus*) to save us constantly repeating the same thing? And could we cope with English weather without the Italians' *umbrella*, which they originally used to give them shade (Latin *umbra*) from the hot sun?

Italy also gave us many words for types of food, like *lasagne, mozzarella, pasta, pizza, spaghetti, tagliatelli* and *zabaglione.*

In fact we have taken many food and drink words from countries where we discovered their particular diet. Sweden gave us the *smorgasbord* (as well as the *ombudsman!*); Hungary lent us *goulash, paprika* and *Tokay*; Mexico introduced us to *burrito, chilli con carne, guacamole, taco* and *tortilla*; and France (the birthplace of *chefs, gourmands* and *gourmets*) gave us the *croissant, fricassée, hors d'oeuvre* and *patisserie,* as well as all those wines named after such French regions as *Bordeaux, Champagne* and *Sauternes.*

Germany loaned us *frankfurter, hamburger, lager* and *sauerkraut.* This last word may remind you that *kraut* is German for "cabbage" and was capitalized as an offensive term for a German.

The increasing popularity of Indian food in Britain is reflected in such loanwords as *biryani, korma, tandoori, vindaloo,* and *jalfrezi* (in Bengali literally "spicy food suitable for someone on a diet").

The English language – like most other languages – reflects social history and world events. As the British Empire grew, we borrowed words from the countries we colonized, taking many from India – including *bungalow* (literally "of Bengal"), *juggernaut* and *shampoo.* From Africa we got *gorilla, voodoo, zebra* and *zombie.* We adopted many Australian words, like *boomerang, budgerigar, didgeridoo, kangaroo, koala* and *wallaby.*

There is a widespread belief that the word *kangaroo* comes from a conversation that someone (perhaps Captain Cook) had with an Aboriginal Australian. The story goes that Cook asked what a particular animal was called and the reply was "kangaroo" which supposedly means "I don't know". However, the word almost certainly comes from an Aboriginal language and is the actual name given to the animal. This is what Captain Cook and Joseph Banks both noted in their 1770 journals, although they spelt it *kangooroo* or *kanguru.*

Another animal whose name we borrowed from its home country is the *teddy bear* – which we got from the USA. It was named after President Theodore ("Teddy") Roosevelt, who went on a famous hunting trip in Mississippi in 1902. Roosevelt was a keen hunter but, when he didn't manage to kill any bears, his guides caught a black bear and tied it to a tree, inviting Theodore to shoot it. Roosevelt refused, saying he would only shoot a bear if it was running free, not tied up.

A cartoon in the *Washington Post* showed Roosevelt refusing to kill a cute little bear cub, with the caption "Drawing the Line in Mississippi". Inspired by the cartoon, Morris Michtom designed a toy bear which he called

"Teddy's Bear". These sold so well that Michtom set up his own toy factory, which was producing more than 100,000 bears by 1938 when Michtom died. A German firm called Steiff also saw the potential and made "teddy bears" for export. Thus the toy came to Britain and eventually became a collectors' item. Someone who loves or collects teddy bears is called an *arctophile* – from Greek *arktos* or Latin *arctos* (= a bear) + the suffix *-phile*.

Our long relationship with North America meant that the Americans used our language (albeit changing it in various ways), and we started employing large numbers of Americanisms. These included such American-Indian words as *chipmunk, moccasin, raccoon, skunk, terrapin* and *totem*, plus newer American coinages like *billboard, movies* and *zipper*.

Two wars with Germany had an effect on the English language. We adopted the surname of Count Ferdinand von Zeppelin to describe airships of the type he invented before World War I. When that war started, Germans could be heard saying "Gott strafe England" – "God punish England" – and we took up the word *strafe*, especially to mean attacking with low-flying aircraft.

World War II accustomed us to loanwords like *blitzkrieg* (German for "lightning war", which we shortened to *blitz*). British planes encountered *flak*, a German word for anti-aircraft fire, taken from letters of their word for pilot-defence-gun: *FLiegerAbwehrKanone.*

But German also gave us such useful words as *angst, hinterland, kitsch, schadenfreude, transvestite* and *zeitgeist*. And we are borrowing a German word when someone sneezes and we say "Gesundheit!" (German for "health").

It may come as a surprise that the term *rainforest* originated in Germany as *Regenwald*, used by Andreas Schimper in a 1898 book, translated in 1903 by W. R. Fisher as *Plant-Geography upon a Physiological Basis*. Mind you, the German word may have been predated by the Swedish *regnskog* and the Danish *regnskov*.

German also gave us the *Rottweiler* – a breed of dog named after Rottweil, a town in south-west Germany.

Talking of dangerous dogs, *Führer* was an innocent German word for "leader" until Hitler chose it as his title when he took over control of Germany in 1934. He actually pinched the idea from Mussolini, who styled himself *Duce* (the Italian word for "leader") more than a decade earlier.

War with Japan meant that we became acquainted with the *kamikaze* – and Japan has continued attacking us with its later inventions: *karaoke, manga* and *sushi. Tsunami* is also a Japanese word, as are those various forms of fighting like *judo, jujitsu, karate* ("empty hand"), *kendo* and *sumo*.

The Cold War meant that we imported Russian vocabulary, including *agitprop, apparatchik, glasnost, gulag* and *perestroika*.

Some people are unhappy about us importing words from elsewhere – especially Americanisms – but all this borrowing has enriched our language. *Weak* is a Germanic word; *feeble* comes from French; and *infirm* comes from Latin. This gives the English three different ways of describing roughly the same thing, but with subtle differences in meaning.

Eponyms

Eponyms are words that derive from people's names. They can come from the name of a real person (*spoonerisms* are named after the absent-minded Warden Spooner of Oxford) or a fictitious character (*malapropisms* get their name from Mrs Malaprop in Sheridan's comedy *The Rivals*).

Eponyms are not as rare as you might think. In fact the English language contains several hundred such words, although we may not immediately recognize them as eponyms. For example, several days of the week are named after people: Tuesday from Tiw or Tyr (the Germanic equivalent of the god Mars); Wednesday from Woden or Odin (the supreme god in Scandinavian mythology – whose name, incidentally, is also commemorated in the town of Wednesbury); Thursday from Thor (another Scandinavian deity); Friday from Frigga (Odin's wife); and Saturday from the Roman god Saturn. Similarly two of our months are named after Roman emperors: July from Julius Caesar and August from Augustus Caesar.

Everyday objects like sandwiches, diesel engines, jacuzzis and Zimmer frames all get their names from their originators. It is fairly easy to guess that some devices – like the Yale lock, the Gallup poll, the Geiger counter and the Celsius thermometer – are named in honour of their inventors, but other words betray their sources less readily.

Did you know that the bacterium *Salmonella* was identified by Daniel Salmon, an American vet? The *decibel* derives from Alexander Graham Bell, inventor of the telephone and the gramophone, whose surname was adapted for the *bel*, a unit measuring the intensity of sound, most familiar in its tenth part, the *decibel*. And the *Elsan* portable toilet comes from the initials of its manufacturer, E. L. Jackson, plus *san*, short for *sanitation*.

Other possibly unexpected eponyms include *America*, named after the explorer Amerigo Vespucci. The *Moog* synthesizer and the *theremin* are both musical instruments named after their inventors: respectively the American Robert Moog and the Russian Lev Theremin. So, too, are the *sousaphone* (from John Philip Sousa, the March King) and the *saxophone* (after the Belgian inventor Adolphe Sax).

A surprisingly large number of English words enshrine the names of French people, including Louis *Braille*, Jules *Leotard*, Etienne de *Silhouette* and Madame de *Pompadour* (whose name is used for a hairstyle). Other French names are embedded in such words as guillotine, magnolia, nicotine and pasteurization. *Chauvinism* immortalises Nicolas Chauvin, a French soldier who thought that Napoleon could do no wrong. And of course *sadism* derives from the Marquis de Sade, although *masochism* comes not from a Frenchman but an Austrian: Leopold von Sacher-Masoch, whose novels described the pleasures of suffering pain.

Quiz 2

Try to identify eponyms from the following clues.

1. These loose-fitting knickers or trousers are named after an American social reformer.
2. This Austrian scientist's name describes the speed of sound.
3. This American cabinet-maker gave his name to a luxurious railway carriage.
4. This Irish land-agent's name is used when somebody refuses contact or trade as a protest.
5. Removing rude words or passages from a book is named after a Scottish doctor.
6. Sir Francis gave his name to a scale of wind speed.
7. This house is named from a girl who was the first person to have her name.
8. This German mathematician's name is applied to a seemingly never-ending surface.
9. He really had a pen-name!
10. An award, named not after me but from Antoinette Perry.

2

Dictionaries

Compiling

Whenever I tell people that I used to be a lexicographer, working on the Oxford dictionaries, they usually ask how compilers decide which words to include in dictionaries.

Most modern dictionaries are based upon usage, so lexicographers need to find out how the language is actually used. When I was at the Oxford University Press, this was done by means of a reading programme. A team of readers, mostly volunteers, ploughed their way through books, magazines and newspapers, looking for examples of new words or interesting citations for old words. Of course, readers had to have (or develop) a feeling for English and what might be new words and phrases.

Naturally we couldn't cover everything printed in English, so we tried to sample all the different kinds of writing: from literary classics to tabloid newspapers; from scientific journals to detective novels; from *The Lancet* to the *New Musical Express*.

The readers copied their finds onto slips of paper, six by four inches, with the illustrated word in the top left-hand corner so that these "cards" could be filed alphabetically.

When the lexicographer came to deal with a particular word, he or she could find a number of cards containing quotations which illustrated the various ways in which the word was used. This basic evidence was supplemented with research in books in the Dictionary Department's own collections and in the invaluable resources of the Bodleian Library and other libraries, including the British Library.

The use of a reading programme was one of the best ideas of the people who started compiling the original *Oxford English Dictionary*. They organized voluntary readers to comb publications in search of useful citations.

Nowadays, the gathering of evidence about the language is much easier because of computerized databases of material, giving lexicographers access to hundreds of examples for particular words.

From the information supplied by such sources as the reading programme, editors had to decide which words deserved inclusion in each particular dictionary. Lexicographers are always aware of the limitations of space. When I compiled the *Oxford Intermediate Dictionary* in the early 1980s, I had room for only 1,200 words, so I had to choose the ones that I thought would be most useful to the readership of children aged between nine and 13. The selection included words that had recently entered the language, like *graffiti, print-out* and *punk*. For larger dictionaries, a useful rule of thumb was that a word is worth considering for inclusion if you have five citations for it from a variety of sources.

People often ask if they can invent a word and get it into the dictionary, but this will only happen if enough people decide to use it, preferably in print. George Orwell's novel *1984* was so influential that his coinages like *doublethink* and *newspeak* entered the language, along with a new sense of *Big Brother*.

When you decide to include a word in a particular dictionary, you then have to ascertain its pronunciation, etymology and the ways in which it is used (for example, if it should be labelled as "slang" or "colloquial"). Compilers of the big *OED* also try to find the earliest possible occurrence of each word in a printed source.

Compiling dictionaries is often likened to painting the Forth Bridge. As soon as you have written a dictionary, it needs updating because the language changes so swiftly. A conservative estimate suggests that three new words enter English every day.

In the 1970s, when I was working on the Supplement to the *OED*, we had to deal with novel words and phrases like *word processor, floppy disc* and *internet* – because it was the start of the computer revolution. The seventies also popularized such new notions as *animal liberation, Sloane Rangers, kneecapping, contraflows* and *tailbacks, Thatcherites, bottle banks* and *E numbers. Labour exchanges* became *job centres*; *family allowances* were replaced by *child benefit*; and the *music centre* superseded the *radiogram*.

Word frequency

What are the most commonly used words in our language? Lexicographers use corpuses (or corpora) to assess which words are used most often. A corpus is a collection of printed, written or spoken material which can be analysed to discover the commonest words.

The Oxford Dictionaries use something called the Oxford English Corpus, which contains a billion words. *The* and *and* are often said to be the commonest words in English and, indeed, *the* tops the OEC list, although *and* is at number 5, with 2, 3 and 4 occupied respectively by *be, to* and *of.*

The word *be* seldom ranks so high in other lists of word frequency: perhaps it scored well in the Oxford list because the compilers lumped it together with related words like *is* and *are.* The presence of the word *to* suggests one of the problems in compiling word frequency lists, as *to* is actually two different words: a preposition (as in "to the bus") and an indicator of an infinitive (as in "To be or not to be"). Some frequency lists distinguish between the two but others lump them together.

Comparing a number of lists, the ten commonest English words appear to be *the, of, and, to, a, in, that, is, was* and *it,* although many lists include *you* and *I* in the top ten.

Corpuses were anticipated by concordances: alphabetical lists of the important words in such writings as the Bible or the works of Shakespeare. In 1630, John Downame published his *Brief Concordance or Table to the Bible* – "serving for the more easie finding out of the most useful places therein conteined". But the best-known biblical index is probably Alexander Cruden's *Complete Concordance to the Holy Scriptures,* which was first published in 1737 and has been continuously in print ever since.

The preface to Mrs Cowden Clark's *Complete Concordance to Shakespeare* (1876) says that she took 16 years to compile it. Of course, she didn't include every single word used by Shakespeare. She points out that *my lord* "as a mere title, occurs in the play of *Hamlet* alone, no fewer than 192 times!"

Later, corpuses were used to create lists of the most common words. In 1843, Joseph Pitman, the pioneer of shorthand, tried to help stenographers by publishing a list of words "showing how often each occurs in 10,000 words, taken from 20 books, 500 from each". Word frequency lists have been used not only in devising forms of shorthand but also in such areas as teaching English – especially to foreigners – where it is useful to know which words the learner may encounter most often.

Word frequency lists can differ widely, depending upon the sources which have been sampled to produce the list. Ernest Horn's *A Basic Writing Vocabulary: 10,000 Words Most Commonly Used in Writing* (1926) was compiled mainly from letters – published and personal.

One of the most famous corpuses is called the Brown Corpus of a million words, developed in the early 1960s by sampling a variety of 2,000-word texts taken from various types of printed material. Many modern corpora use spoken English as well as printed and written sources.

Hartvig Dahl's *Word Frequencies of Spoken American English* describes a corpus assembled from verbatim reports of psychoanalytic cases. This understandably found some words (like *hour* and *analysis*) occurring twice as often as in the Brown Corpus. But the focus on spoken English meant that *I* topped the list, while *uh* occurred 14,000 times (as distinct from six in Brown) and *ah* figured 1936 times (only 22 in Brown).

Computers have made it much easier to assemble corpuses, which are proving invaluable to dictionary-makers who can see how words are used in different contexts and judge how commonly they occur in the language. Search engines like Google offer a simple form of corpus, since you can key in a word and see how frequently it occurs. For instance, at the time of writing, if I key in the word *the*, it produces 9,320 million results; *and* occurs 8,480 million times; while *time* appears 2,490 million times. *Oxford* scores 105 million appearances, while *Cambridge* occurs 93 million times.

The Oxford analysis of word frequency underlines some aspects of modern society. Whereas *man* is in seventh place in the list of nouns, *child* is twelfth and *woman* is 14th. *War* is number 49 but *peace* is not in the top 100. Some words have high rankings because they have multiple meanings (like *way* and *case*) while others like *thing* and *hand* are high up because they occur in many popular phrases (*do your own thing, hand in hand,* etc.).

The commonest words are what you might call the connective tissue of language: short words like *to, of* and *in* which tend to hold our speech together. And most of these words have Anglo-Saxon roots: words that existed before the Normans invaded in 1066.

Swallowing the dictionary

Having worked at compiling dictionaries for more years than I care to remember, I am aware of some of their weaknesses as well as their strengths. One weakness common to most dictionaries is that they explain idioms and phrases less comprehensively than they explain words. If you look up a word in a dictionary, it will usually tell you where it originated, but dictionaries are less helpful when it comes to groups of words. Opening the *Concise Oxford Dictionary* (*COD*) at random, I find this entry: "*Little Russian*, former term for *Ukrainian*". There is no explanation of why Ukrainians were called "Little Russians". Were they smaller than other Soviet people, or was the Ukraine known as "Little Russia"?

The same dictionary tells us that a *Genoa cake* is "a rich fruit cake with almonds on top" but fails to explain its connection with the Italian city of Genoa. A *joss stick* is defined as "a thin stick of a fragrant substance, burnt as incense" but gives us no idea where the "joss" comes from.

This sort of failing in dictionaries is at its worst when it comes to colloquial phrases and proverbs. For example, under *bird*, the *COD* includes seven phrases but explains the origin of only one of them (*do one's bird*, meaning to serve a prison sentence, apparently comes from *birdlime* used as rhyming slang for "time"). Most people can work out for themselves why *the bird has flown* means "the person one is looking for has escaped or left" but will still be puzzled as to why *have a bird* means "be shocked or agitated" in North America, and why *flip someone the bird* is slang for "stick one's middle finger up at someone as a sign of contempt or anger".

Some phrases understandably remain unexplained because their origin is obscure. No dictionary seems able to discover where *in a jiffy* comes from. The *COD*'s entry for *kick the bucket* says curtly: "*informal* die", without giving either of the two commonest explanations for the phrase. Both are gruesome. The most likely is the one that points to *bucket* being used in Norfolk for the beam from which a pig was hung up by the heels to be slaughtered. As the pig struggled, it kicked the "bucket" and eventually died. The other possibility is that the phrase refers to someone committing suicide by standing on a bucket, putting a noose around his neck, and kicking the bucket away.

And what about the phrase *to mind your Ps and Qs*? The *COD* supplies one explanation: "said by some to refer to the care a young pupil must pay in differentiating the tailed letters *p* and *q*". Yet this is only one of a number of possibilities. Some people suggest that the phrase refers to the care needed by a typesetter, picking out metal type from a tray and having to recognize the letters even though they appear reversed. Other less convincing suggestions are that the phrase refers to pub landlords taking care not to confuse pints and quarts when estimating an amount of beer used, or that it is a short way of saying "remember to say please (Ps) and thank you ('kews)". The origin is further confused by one of the *OED*'s illustrative quotations spelling it "to mind your peas and cues" – as if it were an exhortation to gardeners to care for their peas and cucumbers!

Another awkward saying is *sling your hook*, which is simply defined by the *COD* as "*Brit. informal* leave". Why should this phrase be used for "leave" or "clear off"? Does it refer (as some suggest) to a sailor raising the ship's anchor and sailing away? Or a fisherman casting his hook into the water (although that suggests he is staying, not leaving). Or should we picture a workman (perhaps a docker or an agricultural labourer) picking up his hook (even slinging it over his shoulder) and moving on to another job? Perhaps it refers to the practice in old music halls where the theatre manager used a long hooked pole to pull unsuccessful performers off the stage. The OED contains evidence of *sling your hook* from as early as 1874, although it obscures matters further by finding the puzzling phrase *sling your Daniel* from 1873.

Dictionaries can be very helpful but I wish they were more forthcoming on the reasons why we refer to "the luck of the Irish"; why someone is "a dab hand" at something; why we hear rumours "on the grapevine"; why we talk about "money for jam" or "going the whole hog" or "blue murder" or "as bold as brass" or "as fit as a fiddle". It is strange that we constantly use mysterious sayings like this without knowing where they come from. I think we should be told.

Spurious words

When I was working on the *Supplement to the Oxford English Dictionary*, I was fascinated by a section tacked onto the end of the final volume of the original OED. It was entitled "List of Spurious Words" and it was a collection of "the more important spurious words (arising chiefly from misprints or misreadings) that have been current in English dictionaries or other books of some authority".

Yes, even dictionaries make mistakes. Writing about Dr Johnson's famous *Dictionary*, James Boswell wrote: "A few of his definitions must be admitted to be erroneous. Thus, Windward and Leeward, though directly of opposite meaning, are defined identically the same way ['towards the wind']...A lady once asked him how he came to define Pastern, the knee of a horse: instead of making an elaborate defence, as she expected, he at once answered, 'Ignorance, Madam, pure ignorance'".

Of course, Dr Johnson is notorious for some of his ironic or wordy definitions, like "*Oats*, a grain, which in England is generally given to horses, but in Scotland appears to support the people" or "*Dross*, the recrement or despumation of metals". Johnson is well-known for his jaundiced view of the dictionary-writer, with his definition of *lexicographer* as "a harmless drudge". But he included a lesser-known jibe at lexicographers in this entry: "*Grubstreet*, originally the name of a street in Moorfields in London, much inhabited by writers of small histories, dictionaries, and temporary poems; whence any mean production is called grubstreet".

The OED's List of Spurious Words suggests that Johnson was not the only lexicographer whose definitions might arouse doubt or ridicule. The OED's list includes *Colophonian*, which some dictionaries defined as "relating to a colophon or the conclusion of a book" when it actually meant an inhabitant of Colophon, a town in Lydia, an ancient region of Asia Minor. The word *epidemic* was mistakenly read as *exidemic* by some lexicographers, because of the similarity of the letters X and P in 16th and 17th century writing. Spurious words like these are often called ghost words and they can get into more than one dictionary, because lexicographers often borrow from one another.

One such word is *abacot* (a corruption of the word *bycoket*, meaning a kind of cap or head-dress), whose strange history is described by the OED thus: "Through a remarkable series of blunders and ignorant reproductions of error, this word appears in modern dictionaries as *abacot*. In Hall's Chron. *a bicocket* appears to have been misprinted *abococket*, which was copied by Grafton, altered by Holinshed to *abococke*, and finally 'improved' by Abraham Fleming to *abacot* (perhaps through an intermediate *abacoc*); hence it was again copied by Baker, inserted in his *Glossarium* by Spelman, and thence copied by Phillips, and so handed down through Bailey, Ash, Todd, etc., to 19th century dictionaries (some of which provide a picture of the 'abacot'), and even inserted in dictionaries of English and foreign languages".

The word *dord* was defined as "density" in the second edition of *Webster's New International Dictionary* (1934) but it was a ghost word arising from a chemistry expert writing on a slip of paper "D or d, cont./density", meaning that D or d should be included as an abbreviation for *density*. The slip included "cont" to indicate that more D abbreviations would be included. "D or d" was taken to be a word, and thus *dord* got into the dictionary and it wasn't noticed for five years.

Non-existent words are sometimes deliberately inserted into dictionaries – either as a joke or to trap anyone illegitimately trying to copy the work. The first edition of the *Collins COBUILD English Language Dictionary* (1987) contained the fictitious word *hink*, defined thus: "If you hink, you think hopefully and unrealistically about something".

The New Oxford American Dictionary (2001) included the word *esquivalience*, which was defined as "the wilful avoidance of one's official responsibilities". When this dictionary entered a second edition in 2005, its Editor (Erin McKean) confessed that there was a non-existent word somewhere in the letter E. She eventually admitted that it was *esquivalience*, which had been entered to protect the copyright of the dictionary, both in book and electronic form.

This trick is also used in encyclopedias, where it is sometimes called a *Mountweazel*, after a fictitious entry for Lillian Virginia Mountweazel in the

New Columbia Encyclopedia (1975). Lillian was purportedly an American photographer well-known for her series of photos of unusual subjects, including New York buses, the cemeteries of Paris, and rural American mailboxes (this last exhibited extensively abroad and published as "Flags Up!"). Her biography also says that she died in 1973 in an explosion while on an assignment for a magazine called *Combustibles*.

In 1903, Rupert Hughes's *The Musical Guide* ended one of its sections by listing a musical instrument called the *zzxjoanw*, which it said was a Maori word for a drum or a fife, pronounced "shaw". This was fairly obviously a hoax, especially if you knew that the Maori language contains no J, X or Z.

3

Punctuation and grammar

Hyphens

Cries of anguish were heard throughout the land when the Editor of the sixth edition of *The Shorter Oxford Dictonary* removed about 16,000 hyphens from words in the dictionary. Ice-cream became ice cream, *make-over* became *makeover*, and *post-modern* became *postmodern*.

The Editor, Angus Stevenson, justified the change by suggesting that informal methods of communication – like emails and texting – are squeezing out the hyphen. He added: "People aren't confident about using hyphens any more; they're not really sure what they are for".

I can imagine some people feeling unsettled by the notion that language should change just because some people don't understand it properly. Yet compound nouns have been losing their hyphens for many years. People used to write *to-day* and *teen-ager*, but the accepted forms are now *today* and *teenager*.

In fact we can be grateful that some uses (or misuses) of the hyphen have already died out. In *Mind the Stop* (1958), G. V. Carey said: "There is (or was until lately) a convention in certain quarters of printing the names of streets etc. as 'Regent-street', 'Portland-place', 'Shaftesbury-avenue', Berkeley-square', and so on". He added: "There are signs that this irritating practice is beginning to decline".

Carey noted that there are usually three stages in the evolution of connected pairs of words. They start as separate words; then they are hyphenated; and finally become a single word. *Lipstick* started out as *lip stick* and then became *lip-stick* before fusing into one word.

Hyphens still have some important roles to play. The SOED Editor agreed that "There are places where a hyphen is necessary, because you can certainly start to get real ambiguity". An example he gave was: "Twenty-odd people came to the party – or was it twenty odd people?"

There is a real difference between "There are no-parking signs in our street" and "There are no parking signs in our street". The *deep-blue sea* is not the same as the *deep blue sea*. And a man–eating shark in an aquarium is different from a man eating shark in a restaurant. My favourite example of ambiguity caused by the lack of a hyphen is "Where is the lost property office?"

Hyphens are also useful to clarify the pronunciation of grouped words. Omitting the hyphen from *co-operative* makes it look as if it is pronounced KOOP–er-rer-tiv. Is it really safe to remove the hyphens from *do-gooder, co-opt, co-worker, get-at-able,* or *state-of-the-art*?

Some groups of words are so long that they would look ridiculous without hyphens. This is certainly the case with long plant-names, like *John–go-to-bed-at-noon, kiss-me-at-the-garden-gate*, and *kiss-me-twice-before-I-rise*, which are all in the OED. Omitting the hyphens from place-names like Wath-upon-Dearne or Wells-next-the-sea would surely be the work of a semiimbecile.

The word *semiimbecile* suggests another valuable use for hyphens: to avoid awkward groupings of letters, as in *breast-stroke, pre-eminent, drip-proof, anti-inflation* and *glow-worm*.

Hyphens are also used to link nouns in apposition (i.e. that are connected in sense as well as grammatically), such as *actor-manager* or *city-state*, where you are describing a person or thing that is two things simultaneously.

Hyphens are still accepted as the normal way to indicate that a word is divided at the end of a printed line. The 1680 publication called *A Treatise of Stops, Points, or Pauses* says: "An hyphen…is used…in words, when a line will not contain the whole word without it be made longer than the rest, which is not convenient".

The end-line hyphen dates back to the Gutenberg Bible of 1455, in which each printed line was the same length, necessitating the division of some words at the end of lines. This practice continues in the large number of publications where the text is "justified" – with straight edges on the right as well as on the left of a block of text.

Of course, this can create its own problems. A correspondence in the *Guardian* pointed out the danger of dividing the word *legend* into *leg-end*. *Notable* can be turned into *not-able* (or *no-table*), while *fatally* can transmute into a *fat ally*. Probably the most hazardous word to split up is *therapist*.

Ronald McIntosh's *Hyphenation* (1990) points out that many faulty word-divisions arise from computer typesetting, which uses ready-made programs. He quotes from the *Buenos Aires Herald* for 7 July 1989, which had such divisions as *sk-ylab, airs-pace, wo-rried* and *bi-llion*, because it was "splitting

English with a Spanish-language program". But he notes that the *Sunday Times* the same year included dubious word-divisions like *Europe-ans, stro-ll, brou-ght* and *ar-eas.*

In 1963, the Mariner I spacecraft was launched from Cape Canaveral on a mission to Venus but started flying erratically, and had to be blown up. A scientist reported: "Somehow a hyphen had been dropped from the guidance program loaded aboard the computer, allowing the flawed signals to command the rocket to veer left and nose down".

Colonic irritation

Since the Editor of the *Shorter Oxford English Dictionary* raised the spectre of the hyphen being used less and less, it has become clear that other forms of punctuation are also under threat. Perhaps the most threatened punctuation mark is the semi-colon.

Its name damns it from the start. It means "half a colon", so you might assume that it is even less important than the colon, which itself is in danger of being neglected. This neglect arises because many people are unsure when the colon or semi-colon should be used.

The semi-colon is valuable as a sort of halfway house between the comma and the full stop. This is most obvious in a sentence that already contains several commas, as here: "For breakfast, I usually have cereal; an egg, either fried, boiled or poached; some toast with jam, marmalade or peanut butter; and a cup of tea, coffee or hot chocolate".

A semi-colon is also useful where a sentence contains a word like *however* or *moreover* (followed by a comma) introducing a new thought: "I wanted to catch the train; however, I had no money".

But perhaps the semi-colon is used most often to separate clauses or phrases which are related or contrasted in some way, and you don't want to use a conjunction like *and* or *but*, as in "Life is real; life is earnest" or "They were tired; they were homesick; they were at the end of their tether".

While the semi-colon indicates a division between two or more ideas or statements, a colon points towards something that follows, like an explanation or a list of things ("To mend a fuse you need the following: a screwdriver, fusewire, a knife..."). In the words of Fowler's *Modern English Usage,* the colon's job is "delivering the goods that have been invoiced in the preceding words". A good example occurs in Bernard Shaw's *Major Barbara*: "Nobody can say a word against Greek: it stamps a man at once as an educated gentleman".

The colon can introduce a quotation – for example "Remember the words of Martin Luther King: 'Injustice anywhere is a threat to justice everywhere'". And it also has the function of separating two contrasting or conflicting phrases, as in "Man proposes: God disposes".

Many people seem unaware of the subtleties in using such punctuation marks as colons and semi-colons. So one might wonder if we need punctuation at all. That question might be answered by contrasting these two sentences: "Charles I walked and talked half an hour after his head was cut off". And "Charles I walked and talked. Half an hour after, his head was cut off".

Certainly the ancient Greeks and Romans managed without punctuation in their early days, but Latin writers from about the 4th century began using a range of marks to clarify texts and indicate pronunciation, especially when reading aloud. By the Middle Ages, this practice was used to help in reciting the Christian liturgy – gospels, lessons, psalms, etc. This is visible in *The Book of Common Prayer*, where the *Psalms* use colons to indicate a pause in reading or singing (for example, "Wash me throughly from my wickedness: and cleanse me from my sin").

In monasteries, scribes writing manuscripts inserted various marks, such as a point high on the line where we would put a comma, and a point low on the line where we would use a full stop. The arrival of printing led gradually to the standardisation of punctuation.

The earliest book entirely about English punctuation – *A Treatise of Stops, Points, or Pauses* (1680) – recommended that, when reading, you should count one when you reach a comma, two at a semi-colon, and four at a colon. Madame Leinstein's *Punctuation in Verse; or, The Good Child's Book of Stops*, published about 1825, disagreed:

> For the *Colon* count *three* – for the *Period, four*,
>
> As, "The robin is dead: he now is no more".

Nowadays, emails and texting seem to be endangering all kinds of punctuation. Yet it will be a pity if many punctuation marks die out – particularly as we have a limited number of them.

Punctuation has some very useful functions. As long ago as 1939, G. V. Carey noted that "Modern usage has tended towards increasing economy in punctuation" but he added that "The first essential is that the meaning of what is written should be conveyed to the reader's mind, through his eye, with the least possible delay and without any ambiguity".

As the Fowler brothers wrote in *The King's English* (1930): "The work of punctuation is mainly to show, or hint at, the grammatical relation between words, phrases, clauses and sentences; but it must not be forgotten that stops also serve to regulate pace, to throw emphasis on particular words and give them significance, and to indicate tone".

Perhaps we need campaigns to keep punctuation marks from falling into disuse. The lexicographer Erin McKean has started a Semicolon Appreciation Society. She has produced T-shirts with a large semicolon on the front and, on the back, the message: "The semicolon is not used enough; the comma is used too often".

Parts of speech

Having asked if we really need punctuation marks (and having answered my own question in the affirmative), I also started wondering if we need parts of speech.

Some of us have been through the agonies of being taught Grammar at school and had to do things like "parsing" to drum into us how to recognize a noun, a verb, an adverb, etc. Writing about his early schooling, Stephen Leacock recalled the experience thus: "We learned by heart, out of a little book called Grammar, the statement that 'There are eight parts of speech, the noun, the pronoun, the adjective, the verb, the adverb, the preposition, the conjunction, and the interjection'. It was just a mass of words. We hadn't the least idea of what a part of speech meant".

Grammarians (and teachers) tend to make sweeping statements about parts of speech . For instance, a 1901 textbook says that the word *adverb* comes from Latin *ad* to and *verbum* word or verb. "So *Adverb = a word added to a verb*". Yet this is not always true – *even* is an adverb in "It was even noisier" but it modifies an adjective, not a verb. And an adverb isn't always a single word: it can be a phrase like "for a while" or "if possible".

Parts of speech are at least useful to lexicographers. You only have to open a dictionary to see words marked as *adj., adv.* and *n.* (the *Oxford English Dictionary* strangely describes a noun as *sb.* – meaning "substantive"). But how useful are these designations?

For instance, I have always wondered about the value of the description "pronoun". Surely it is just a kind of noun, not a part of speech in its own right? In the sentence "The man panicked, and he ran away", *man* and *he* both refer to the same person, so why do they need two different parts of speech? Besides, a pronoun can represent a whole phrase, not just a noun. Randolph Quirk's *Grammar* (1985) gives the example: "*The man* invited *the little Swedish girl* because *he* liked *her*". In this case, the pronouns *he* and *her* represent phrases of two and four words respectively.

Parts of speech are really only labels for categories, which can fluctuate a great deal. Many words can be used as different parts of speech. The word *Sunday* is normally classed as a noun, but it serves as an adverb in the exchange: "When are you going?" "Sunday". The word *round* can be a noun, adjective, verb, adverb and preposition – as well as sometimes serving as a suffix.

How did we get the idea of "parts of speech"? In India as well as Greece around the first century BC, scholars began to analyse language. The Greek grammarian Dionysius Thrax decided that there were eight parts of speech: noun, verb, participle, article, pronoun, preposition, adverb and conjunction. This idea was adapted into Latin, although grammarians made the interjection separate from the adverb (where the Greeks had placed it) and excluded the article (which doesn't exist in Latin). The same categories were transferred from Latin into English.

One of the earliest publications about English grammar – William Bullokar's *Pamphlet for Grammar* (1586) – listed the same eight parts of speech as Dionysius Thrax, except that he replaced Thrax's "article" with "interjection". Like Thrax, he omits the adjective but refers to a "noun-adjective" (like *black* or *hard*) and later calls this simply an adjective.

Ben Jonson's *English Grammar* (1640) says: "In our English speech, we number the same parts with the Latins: Noun, Pronoun, Verb, Participle, Adverb, Conjunction, Preposition, Interjection. Only, we add a ninth, which is the Article [*the* and *a*]". Note that Jonson also omits the adjective.

There are still disputes as to how many parts of speech there are. Some people would add extra designations, such as the numeral (two, twice, third), and others would regard the participle (having, being) as a verb, not a separate part of speech. Other grammarians avoid using the phrase "parts of speech" altogether and instead call these things "word classes" or even "grammatical (or lexical) categories".

In *English Grammatical Categories* (1970), Ian Michael estimated that, up to the year 1800, "Grammarians gave their approval to 56 different systems of parts of speech".

Parts of speech are supposed to help us identify what function a word serves, but the variety of categories can be confusing. The confusion may be further complicated by the many other terms that grammarians use – like mood, case, number, gender, tense, gerunds, prefixes and suffixes, comparatives and superlatives. Even if the concept of parts of speech has its uses, it still leaves us uncertain what part of speech to assign to such words as *yes, no, not,* or *very.* Is *alone* an adjective or adverb? Is *five* a noun or an adjective? What part of speech is *however* – or *whatever*?

David Crystal wrote: "Any classification of words which raises so many problems is clearly suspect". I am inclined to agree.

4

Spelling

A bad spell

Spelling is a contentious issue in Britain, probably because the English language is particularly hard to spell. English is inconsistent because it arose from a combination of several different languages.

Italians don't appear to have spelling contests, since Italian words tend to be spelt as they are pronounced. But in Britain we have numerous problems caused by such things as the same sound being spelt with a variety of different letters. For example, the sound of a long E is spelt EE in *seem* but it can be spelt in many other ways, as in the words *he, ream, protein, people, key, ski, fiend, debris* and *quay*. The sound of a short letter I is spelt one way in *bit* but differently in *pretty, women* and *system*. There are 13 ways of spelling the "sh" sound, as in *short, sugar, issue, mansion, fission, ration, suspicion, ocean, conscious, chaperon, schist, fuchsia* and *pshaw*. And what about that confusing pair: *their* and *there*?

The converse of this problem is that some letters represent a range of different sounds. Foreigners trying to learn English may be puzzled by the fact that *mother* and *bother* look as if they rhyme but don't. Perhaps the best-known anomaly is in the letters OUGH, which can be pronounced in a surprising number of different ways, represented by words in this rhyme:

Though the tough cough and hiccough plough me through,

O'er life's dark lough my course I still pursue.

All these difficulties feed the clamour for spelling reform. This is the aim of bodies like the Simplified Spelling Society. However, as this society recognizes, "the great difficulty of arriving at any agreement is the multiplicity of possible systems". The Simplified Spelling Society itself lists six such systems which it prefers: SoundSpel, Cut Spelling, Freespeling, Stage 1, New Spelling and Saispel.

In fact, people have been trying to reform English spelling since the 16th century. The American lexicographer Noah Webster listed many previous schemes, such as those of Benjamin Franklin (who wanted to abolish the letters C, J, Q, W, X and Y) and a certain Mr Elphinstone who "published a treatise in a very ridiculous orthography" (including sentences like "Evvery tung is independent ov every oddher"). Webster favoured spelling reform and he simplified many spellings in his famous dictionary in the early 19th century. This explains why Americans use spellings like *color, favor, plow, theater* and *check* (where we use *cheque*). Many of Webster's proposals didn't catch on, such as changing *feather* into *fether* and *thumb* into *thum*.

Yet Webster admitted that English spelling is a mess not only because of the language's chequered history but also because of "the changes to which the pronunciation of a language is liable". He notes that the K in *know* and *knave* used to be sounded. This implies that a system of simplified spelling would have to be changed as pronunciation changes.

In any case, changing spelling to match pronunciation would be difficult in English, as pronunciation is not uniform throughout Britain. Some people pronounce the A in *bath* like the "ar" in *card*, and others like the "a" in *cat*, while *right* can be heard as *ryt* or *reet*. In East Anglia they apparently pronounce *beauty* as "booty".

While many of us pronounce the word *off* as it is written, posh people as well as Cockneys pronounce it as "orf". Cockneys also turn the double T in *butter* into a glottal stop, pronouncing the word as "bu—er". Many people pronounce the letter H as "haitch", which sounds alien to those of us who say "aitch". Bernard MacLaverty's story *Walking the Dog* includes an episode where IRA gunmen insist on hearing how a prisoner pronounces H, because that ostensibly reveals if someone is Protestant or Catholic.

Spelling reform is rendered considerably more difficult by the fact that English is now a world language – spoken by perhaps ten per cent of the world's people. It would be virtually impossible to co-ordinate reforms covering the diverse forms of English spoken in the USA, Australia, South Africa, the Caribbean, etc. However, this has not stopped people trying to reform our spelling.

Spelling reform

Proposals for spelling reform have continued to multiply, despite the difficulties involved. As long ago as 1712, Jonathan Swift attacked "the foolish opinion advanced of late years that we ought to spell exactly as we speak".

Most public libraries classify books according to the Dewey Decimal Classification System, which was devised by Melville Dewey, a fierce advocate of simplified spelling. Dewey simplified his own first name to Melvil, and his library handbook uses his reformed system of spelling. In 1930, R. E. Zachrisson proposed a revised form of English called Anglic, containing 27 consonant symbols and 27 vowel symbols. His magazine *Anglic* was described as an "Eduekaeshonal Revue". Translating Hamlet's most famous soliloquy into Anglic would give lines like this:

> Whedher 'tis noebler in the miend to sufer
> The slingz and aroz of outraejus fortuen,
> Or to taek armz against a see of trublz,
> And by opoezing end them.

Bernard Shaw, a keen champion of spelling reform, left money in his will for the development of a new alphabet. In 1958, Shaw's executors organized a competition, which was won by Kingsley Read with an alphabet consisting of four types of letters which looked nothing like the alphabet we know and love. Penguin Books published an edition of Shaw's *Androcles and the Lion* using the old and new alphabets but nothing really came of it.

Spelling reforms have been agreed in several countries (e.g. France, Spain and Germany) but these have often been ignored – or even reversed when they failed to gain wide recognition. In 1740, the Académie Française changed the spelling of one-third of French words – for instance, by substituting accents for an unstressed S, changing *estoit* to *étoit* and *boiste* to *boîte*. These alterations were accepted, but proposed changes in Germany have had a rougher ride. A simplified spelling system was instituted in Germany in 1998, splitting some compounds into two or more parts and replacing the old double S (which looks like an overweight letter B) with "ss" in some words but not all. However, famous authors like Gunter Grass refused to allow their books to be printed with the new spellings. Influential publications like *Die Welt* and *Der Spiegel* ditched the new orthography and reverted to the old.

One method of reform that seemed likely to succeed was the Initial Teaching Alphabet, which was introduced into many British schools in 1961 as an experiment. The ITA was developed by Sir James Pitman from his grandfather's Phonotypy and a system called Nue Speling. It used 44 characters, including 17 vowels, to represent sounds and was intended as a transitory stage to lead children into "normal" reading, where about half the words are spelt differently.

ITA appeared to increase many pupils' literacy but it never became a mainstream option, perhaps because it presented several problems. One teacher said that some children found it hard to make the transition from ITA to "normal" spelling. Other teachers were worried about children using ITA at school but encountering traditional spelling everywhere else. ITA's popularity declined thereafter.

One flaw in ITA is that people don't normally read by spelling out the words but by recognising them – usually through experience gained from previous reading. Good spelling (in whatever system) depends on familiarity gained from seeing words in print. This idea was corroborated by a survey which found that many more children can spell familiar words like *Hogwarts* (Harry Potter's school) than unfamiliar ones like *Edinburgh* or *parliament*.

As with most other aspects of language, spelling is more likely to change through the usage of ordinary people than by any imposed system. For example, text messaging has already had the effect of reforming some people's spelling habits, transforming "See you later" into "C U L8R" and introducing such shortenings as *spk, yr* and *gt* (speak, your and get or got).

Personally, I am against spelling reform, because I believe – in the words of Mark Twain – that it would "substitute one inadequacy for another". Mind you, Mark Twain claimed: "I myself am a Simplified Speller. I belong to that unhappy guild that is patiently and hopefully trying to reform our drunken old alphabet by reducing his whiskey. Well, it will improve him. When they get through and have reformed him all they can by their system, he will be only HALF *drunk*. Above that condition their system can never lift him. There is no competent, and lasting, and real reform for him but to take away his whiskey entirely".

Spelling bees

The Dicos d'Or is a peculiarly French tradition. It is an annual spelling contest, run by *Lire* magazine since 1985. Contestants have to qualify for the final in a series of regional rounds. Competitors try to write down correctly a dictated passage which contains some difficult spellings. A recent winner was a secondary-school maths teacher who made only one mistake.

The Dicos d'Or suggests how seriously the French take their language, although we already knew about this trait from such things as the fuss they made about "Franglais" corrupting their language, and the institution of the Académie Française, which was set up in 1635 by Cardinal Richelieu (whose name, I notice, seems to mean "Rich place"). The Académie's task is to regulate the French language, even though experience shows that controlling a language is virtually impossible.

Yet a contest like the Dicos d'Or is in the venerable tradition of spelling contests, dating back more than a century. Spelling bees became popular in 19th-century America, where the word "bee" had long been used to describe any social get-together to do something useful. "Spinning bee" is found as early as 1769, and Americans also assembled for quilting bees, husking bees, logging bees and (sadly) lynching bees. I still like to think that this use of the word "bee" derives from the activity resembling a beehive, although some etymologists cast doubt on this derivation.

The American tradition continues undaunted, with the finals of the National Spelling Bee (for children under 15) held annually in Washington. The champions in a dozen recent contests won because they knew how to spell these words: *chiaroscurist, logorrhea, demarche, succedaneum, prospicience, pococurante, autochthonous, appoggiatura, Ursprache, serrefine, guerdon* and *Laodicean*.

Like crosswords, spelling bees came to Britain as a craze from the USA. BBC Radio included spelling quizzes on *Children's Hour* in the 1930s, and I remember spelling bees from my schooldays. But that was many years ago, and spelling bees seem to have been widely supplanted by general-knowledge tests: games like Trivial Pursuit when we are at home, and pub quizzes when we go out.

However, Britons can still become heated when they encounter misspellings – notably on those occasions when they notice a greengrocer advertising "Tomatos" or "Tomato's" or even "Tomatoe's". Former American vice-president Dan Quayle notoriously made a fool of himself on a school visit, telling a student that *potato* should be spelt potatoe. This was not the only spelling error perpetrated by Quayle. His 1989 Christmas card expressed the hope "May our nation continue to be the beakon (*sic*) of hope to the world", and some of his headed notepaper at the White House said "Office of the Vice President…The Council on Competativeness (*sic*)". In his defence, Dan Quayle quoted Mark Twain's dictum that "You should never trust a man who has only one way to spell a word". Unfortunately this aphorism was uttered not by Mark Twain but by President Andrew Jackson.

Some people might support Dan Quayle in ending potato with -oe, since that is the spelling recommended for the sound of "toe" in the Initial Teaching Alphabet. However, if he had consistently followed the ITA, Quayle should have spelt potato as poetaetoe. In fact someone has suggested that the proper spelling of potato is GHOUGHPHTHEIGHTTEEAU, if the P is sounded like the GH in hiccough, the O is pronounced like the OUGH in dough, the T like the PHTH in phthisis, the A like the EIGH in neighbour, the T like the TTE in gazette, and the final O like the EAU in plateau!

Artificial languages

There are an estimated four to five thousand languages in the world – enough, you might think, for anyone wishing to communicate with their fellow humans. Yet this doesn't stop people inventing new languages of their own.

Charles K. Ogden's aim was to improve communication when he introduced Basic English in 1930. Ogden said it would take seven years to learn English, seven months to learn Esperanto but only seven weeks for Basic English. He stripped down English vocabulary to 850 words: 400 of them general words for things (like *air, animal* and *art*); 200 for what he called "picturable" words (e.g. *apple, clock, toe*); 100 for "operations" like *come, go, the* and *not*; 100 for general qualities like *angry, fat* and *serious*; and 50 for "opposite qualities" like *cruel, rough* and *sad*.

This simplified language was designed to be easily assimilated by foreigners but it has the drawbacks of other limited wordlists, such as omitting common English words like today, whether and world. Its simplicity might be expected to encourage plain usage but ideas actually take longer to express in Basic because you have to use roundabout expressions. For example, where normal English might use the word *inescapable*, Basic has to say something like "from which there is no getting away". Winston Churchill was reportedly an enthusiast for Basic English until someone pointed out that Basic would translate his famous phrase "blood, toil, tears and sweat" into "blood, hard work, eyewash and body water".

I discovered for myself the limitations of stripped-down wordlists when I undertook to translate a couple of English books into texts for foreign learners (OUP's "Alpha" series), using only 1500 words from a specified list. This made it virtually impossible to retain the subtleties in a book like P. G. Wodehouse's *Summer Lightning*, where one incident included the theft of a set of false teeth. False teeth were not included in the list of acceptable words, so I had to substitute the theft of a pair of spectacles.

One might argue that Basic English is unnecessary, except as a learning tool, because English itself has become a world language. However, some people worry that this may represent a form of English imperialism, and that it is better to create an entirely new, neutral language for use throughout the world, mainly as a second language. The most successful attempt at this is undoubtedly Esperanto. A conservative estimate suggests that Esperanto is spoken by two million people, although some claim as many as 15 million. Even this sounds less impressive if we remember that the world probably contains nearly 7,000 million people.

Esperanto was invented in the 19th century by Ludovic Zamenhof, born in 1859 in Bialystock, now part of Poland but at that time under Russian rule. Zamenhof witnessed the ethnic feuding around him and decided that an international language might help to resolve these conflicts. He created Esperanto with a simple structure based on root words whose senses could be changed with affixes. He drew the vocabulary mainly from European languages, including German, Russian and Latin, which means that many of the words are recognisable to Europeans.

Perhaps the most useful artificial language is Braille, devised by Louis Braille – a Frenchman who was himself blind. It enables unsighted people to read by means of a grid of six raised dots which indicate letters of the alphabet and even whole words. It is an astonishingly simple idea, although I discovered its complexities when I volunteered to transcribe books into Braille and had to impress the dots correctly onto thick paper. One mistake meant that you had to start the whole page again. But Braille enables a practised user to read an average of two words per second simply by touch. A similar invention for the blind is Moon type, devised by William Moon in 1845, which employs actual embossed letters of the alphabet and may therefore be easier than Braille for people to learn if they lose their sight late in life.

Of course, there are also numerous artificial languages invented by writers for use in books, television series, etc. – like those concocted by J. R. R. Tolkien for *The Lord of the Rings*. As early as 1726, Jonathan Swift in *Gulliver's Travels* invents words like *Tramecksan* and *Slamecksan* to describe the two warring parties in Lilliput. The Klingon language devised for *Star Trek* has been described as "guttural, choppy and atonal" as well as "unpleasant to the ear", yet Trekkies are fascinated by this language, which can even be studied through conversation tapes. And devotees have translated *Hamlet* into Klingon!

Text messages

I said above that text messaging is changing many people's spelling. It was a fairly new phenomenon when I wrote a Wordplay article about it in 2002, but now it seems that most of the population is sending text messages. For those unfamiliar with texting, these are messages sent by using telephone keypads. On many phones, the keys for each number from 2 to 9 also allow you to key in particular letters of the alphabet: 2 covers ABC, 3 covers DEF, and so on. Thus you can spell out words by pressing the keys the correct number of times (press number 2 twice for the letter B, three times for the letter C). For instance, you can send the word *faced* by pressing 333-2-222-33-3.

As most mobile phones have keys much smaller than people's fingers, it's easy to press the wrong key and send the word *death* instead of *debug*, *apron* instead of *arson*, *oaths* instead of *maths*, *carnage* instead of *barmaid*, or *boobs* instead of *bombs*.

Different words created by pressing the same keys are commonly called "textonyms". This gives rise to a game in which people list as many words as they can produce by pressing a particular set of keys. For instance, if you press the second, sixth and ninth keys, you can get nine different possibilities: *Amy, any, bow, box, boy, cow, cox, coy* or *coz*. You might even look for appropriate sets of such words. For example, pressing 5477 can give you *kiss* or *lips*, while 4633 gives you *good* or *home*.

Text messaging only allows for short messages, so text messagers have taken to using many abbreviations and symbols, virtually creating a new language. This employs many devices to shorten words: for example, creating words from letters of the alphabet, so that B represents *be*, C represents *see* and NE is used for *any*. Numbers are also used to abbreviate words – as in B4 (for before) and L8R (*later*). The number 2 can mean *two* or *to* or *too* (and presumably a ballet-dancer can wear a 22). Text messages tend to achieve brevity by omitting a large number of letters (especially vowels) from words, so that *anything* becomes NTHING, *weekend* becomes WKND and *text messaging* turns into TXT MSGING.

Punctuation marks can be made into what are called "emoticons" – pictures which convey an emotion or mood. Many of these depend on the reader turning them on their side – at an angle of 90 degrees – so that a cheerful face is represented by :-) or :->, while :-(or :-< depicts a sad face.

Even if you don't possess a mobile phone, you can try your hand at text messaging by translating sentences or even poems into text speak (or TXT SPK). You might start with Hamlet's famous soliloquy: 2B OR NT 2B, and continue with a Bill Haley song: CUL8R ALIG8R.

Technology has also come up with "predictive texting", which supposedly anticipates the words you want to send. When you press a number key once, it predicts the word you intend to send. Thus *faced* can be texted by pressing no more than 3-2-2-3-3, which entails half the keystrokes you would have used in the earlier example.

This can theoretically save time but it may actually add to the effort of sending a message. If you want to type the word *concert* for example, the most commonly-used text system predicts that you want to say *concept* – and you have to change that word into the one you actually want. Similarly, predictive texting can turn *love* into *loud* and *too* into *two* or *tom*.

Predictive texting was anticipated by the spell-checker, which is provided with most computers and ostensibly saves you time by checking how you spell each word. It can certainly help you to avoid such common mistakes as typing *hte* when you mean *the*. However, it cannot help if you use homonyms, typing *of coarse* when you mean *of course*, or *diffuse* when you mean *defuse*, as the "wrong" words are still acceptable to a spell-checker.

And a spell-checker can introduce errors of its own. Many spell-checkers are American, and instruct you to spell *theatre* as *theater* and *behaviour* as *behavior*. When I typed the word *cox* earlier, the word was highlighted to show that it isn't included in my computer's spell-check dictionary, which offers me the alternative suggestions of *Cox* (with a capital C), *coax, co, cocks* and *cod*. When I was writing a television review, I wanted to say that a programme was *watchable* but the spell-checker would only allow *patchable* or *washable*. And it couldn't cope with the French philosopher Diderot, offering instead: *Demerit, Desert, Idiot, Deirdre* and *Diego*!

The problems caused by spell-checkers are admirably illustrated in a poem which begins thus:

> I have a spelling chequer,
> It came with my Pea Sea.
> It plane lee marks four my revue
> Miss steaks aye can knot sea.
>
> Eye ran this poem threw it,
> Your sure reel glad two no.
> It's vary polished in it's weigh,
> My chequer tolled me sew.
>
> A chequer is a bless sing,
> It freeze yew lodes of thyme.
> Hit helps me right awl stiles two reed,
> And aides me when aye rime.

Grammar checkers can also be misleading. A survey showed that a typical grammar checker supplied with a computer only detected 19 out of 67 grammatical errors but labelled many correct sentences as errors. As with spell-checkers, you have to be careful about weighing up the advice you are given, which sometimes seems unnecessarily finicky (as when grammar checkers advise you to avoid the passive voice on almost every occasion). If I write "A rose by any other name…", the grammar checker in my computer would want me to give the quotation in full, instead of assuming that the reader will recognize the reference.

Another possible source of confusion is provided by computer thesauruses, which offer alternatives that some people (especially foreign learners of English) may assume can be substituted directly for another word. The thesaurus on my computer suggests that I could have started this paragraph by saying "Another probable spring" or "Another likely font".

5

Foreign parts

Idiotic idioms

If the English language's quaint spelling can confuse foreigners, they may also be puzzled by English idioms. Idioms are particularly important for foreign learners, who have to familiarize themselves with such puzzling idioms as *clean as a whistle, the name of the game* and *apple-pie order*. A newly-arrived visitor to Britain might well be bewildered if you told him not to beat about the bush or asked him if you were both singing from the same hymn-sheet.

Such idiomatic phrases don't mean exactly what a learner might assume they ought to mean. How could an innocent foreigner be expected to know the figurative nature of "kick the bucket", which was underlined by a joke in the film *It's a Mad Mad Mad Mad World*, where a dying man's foot shoots out and actually kicks a bucket?

Foreign learners sometimes give themselves away by misusing idioms, which present problems because their significant words cannot usually be replaced by others. Thus a foreigner familiar with the idiom "beat about the bush" might think he could say "hit about the bush" or "beat about the shrub". Our language allows him to describe a diversionary tactic as a red herring but not a pink herring or a red mullet. He can say that someone gave up the ghost but not that the ghost was given up by that person.

It is a common source of amusement for native speakers to quote examples of cases where foreign learners slip up because they are unfamiliar with particular idioms. Gerard Hoffnung famously did this in his speech at the Oxford Union in 1958, quoting publicity from Tyrolean hoteliers writing such things as "I am amazing diverted by your entreaty for a room" and "Sorrowfully I cannot abide your auto". The BBC's Far Eastern service allegedly assembled such oddities as "You are very invited to take advantage of the chambermaid" and (from a notice at the entrance to a temple) "It is forbidden to enter a woman. Even a foreigner if dressed as a man".

One can sympathize with foreign learners because one knows how hard it is for us Brits to get used to the idioms in foreign languages. For example, if you are trying to learn French, your experience of French restaurants may tell you that *sauce à la maître d'hôtel* is melted butter with parsley and lemon juice, but how are you to guess that *poisson d'avril* is not a fish caught in April but a joke played on April Fool's Day, and *tirer le diable par la queue* doesn't mean "to pull the devil by the tail" but to be hard up or to live from hand to mouth.

Sometimes you can guess the meaning of an idiom because it corresponds with one in your own language. The British "Birds of a feather flock together" is similar to the French "Qui se ressemble, s'assemble" and the German "Gleich und gleich gesellt sich gern". A Portuguese phrase which might be comprehensible to English learners is *Aquas passadas não movem moinhos*, which means "Waters that have passed don't drive mills" – reminiscent of our own proverbs about water under the bridge and even spilt milk. But what are we to make of the Portuguese *Armar-se em carapau de corrida* which literally means "He is like a racing mackerel"?

Phrase books

Phrase books are supposed to help people speak a foreign language. However, many phrase books mangle the language so disastrously that they are laughable rather than helpful.

The worst phrase book of all – *The New Guide of the Conversation, in Portuguese and English* (1855) – was full of such solecisms as "That pond it seems me many multiplied of fishes" and "This meat ist not too over do".

It is fun to read collections of these weird phrases but it is more satisfying to find them for yourself. My own collection includes a brochure which I got in Norway, which says "Here is a lot of paths for walkings in the mountains" and a booklet from Belgium stating that "The festival features seven shows of encounters orbiting the theme of light, colour, the moment". When I played a round of mini-golf in Belgium, the score-card warned me: "Those persons whose behaviour would become a nuisance the others, will be invited to leave the course, without reimburse of the prise of their tickets".

During the First World War, many phrase books were published to assist British soldiers with the unfamiliar French language. Frank Scudamore's *"Parley Voo"!!* – published in 1915 and subtitled "Practical French phrases and how to pronounce them, for daily use by British soldiers", includes the

French words for "gripe draught", "stirrup leathers" and "a surcingle", reminding us that horses were widely used in this war. Scudamore also helps Tommies to sing *The Marseillaise,* transliterating it as:

Al-longs, ong-fong der lar Part-ree-e-yer,

Ler joor der glwore ait arr-ee-vay.

Hubert Dupont's *The British-American Soldiers' English-French Conversation Guide* (1919) includes the French equivalents for "American expressions and colloquialisms", such as:

boodle	pillage
buggy	voiture or fiacre
dinkie	très chic
dude	un fat
a mug (foolish person)	bête
I'm tickled	je suis très content

While these phrase books conjure up the spirit of an age, others show themselves up by being conspicuously out-of-date. As late as 1945, the *English-French Dictionary and Phrase book* was including such archaic items as fowling-piece, gas-pendant, inverted mantle, napery, pen-wipe and rush-light.

The preface of a text-book published in 1967 for foreign students of English claimed that "This edition has required some considerable revision to bring it quite up to date." That archaic use of "quite" may put you on your guard, as the word was surely not used *quite* like that in the 1960s.

The book describes British television (on which you can see "lively one-act plays, comic turns, and amusing episodes of all sorts"); our telephones ("I then clock the number, that is, I turn the dial with my finger for the telephone number of the place I want"); and our capital city ("Pardon me, sir, but am I right for the Marble Arch?").

The author tells us that "When I wish to visit one of my intimate friends, I do not take the trouble to inform him beforehand, but I go to his house, and ring the bell. Someone comes to the door: it is the maid." Then follows this conversation between the author and his friend:

Harry Hallo, John, is it you? (I am) delighted to see you....

John Would you care to come with me to the theatre next Wednesday?

Harry What's on?

John "Saint Joan".

Harry By whom (is it written)?

John By Bernard Shaw. They say it is his best play. It is a splendid piece.

Conversations are often the weakest part of phrase books. They tend to sound artificial – or even surreal. W. G. Hartog's *Brush Up Your French,* published by the *Daily Mail* in 1930, has the following conversation between a French couple about the weather:

M. D. What beastly weather!

Mme D. Yes, indeed. It has been like this now for four days. Wind, rain and hail. It's a long time since we have had such stormy weather.

M. D. What does the Meteorological Office say about it? Let's see the evening paper. By Jingo! It's not very reassuring. There is a deep depression over the Channel which shows a tendency to move southwards. Such a condition of barometric pressure will bring along north-easterly winds over the whole of Northern France. There will be frost at night, probably more severe than hitherto. The bad weather will continue.

Mme D. Well, we shall have to go out as little as possible.

M. D. It's disgusting. Mathieu and I had decided to go tomorrow to see the big Rugger match at Colombes.

Phrase books like this may make you doubt the wisdom of Sir Francis Galton, who wrote in *The Art of Travel* (1867): "Recollect to take with you vocabularies of all the tribes whom you are at all likely to visit".

Getting by and getting off

A visit to St Petersburg spurred me to try learning some basic Russian.

My attitude to learning languages for use on trips abroad is summed up in the title of a well-known series of phrase books: "Get By in French" (or German or Swahili). I just want to know enough to get by, without too many misunderstandings or embarrassments. I need to know basic words like yes, no, please, thank you and excuse me. And I particularly want to learn such essential foreign phrases as "Can you speak English?" (the perfect "Get By" solution if the answer is yes). It's also useful to know phrases like the one I found indispensable in Germany: "Noch ein Bier, bitte" (another beer, please).

As previously noted, phrase books and language courses are notorious for listing expressions we are never likely to use. *Take Off in Russian* (OUP) offers such useful phrases as "There are no more carrots", "I was frightened of myself", "She is turning 65" and "I hope it's not Wagner". *Teach Yourself Instant Russian* promises to teach you Russian in six weeks, although this includes learning such unlikely phrases as "River so beautiful in the sun", "My house is too big" and "To eat much red meat is harmful".

Nowadays you can even find collections of foreign phrases on the internet, although I am dubious about the Master Russian website which offers the sentence: "I am living in room number 101", conjuring up disturbing memories of George Orwell's *1984*.

Some phrase books assisted my basic understanding of Russian, although they often made me plough through pages of irrelevant material to find what I wanted. The Berlitz *Russian for Travellers* hid the phrases I wanted amongst unnecessary sayings like "How's life?" and "through the forest". Hugo's *Russian Phrase Book* was much more helpful, starting with yes, no, thank you and please, plus other useful expressions like "Sorry!" and "Where is the toilet?"

Mind you, the Hugo booklet hardly encouraged optimism about my Russian visit by saying things like "Standards of service, courtesy and cleanliness vary but, compared to those of Western European hotels, are not likely to be more than adequate". This is another problem with phrase books: they may quickly go out-of-date, like the Berlitz guide which informs you that Intourist or Sovincentr will tell you the Russian hotel where you are permitted to stay.

Some phrase books try to show they are up-to-the-minute by including chat-up lines to help you communicate with attractive foreigners. There have always been jokes about Britishers saying to Parisians "Voulez-vous coucher avec moi?" but this sort of communication is unlikely to have actually appeared in old-fashioned phrase books. Nowadays the Lonely Planet books even include lines like "Oh baby, don't stop", although it is hard to visualize these being uttered with phrase book in hand. The Berlitz Russian guide is more circumspect, offering fairly innocent lines like "Would you like to go for a walk?" and "May I take you home?" Hugo's *Russian Phrase Book* never gets so personal, merely offering suitable expressions to use when talking to a business associate – like "Our product is selling very well in the UK market" and "There are good government grants available".

The most unashamed phrase book I have seen is Jay De Leon's *Love Talk in Five Languages*, subtitled "The essential phrase book for the romantic traveller". It tells you the French, German, Spanish and Italian for such expressions as "Do you snore?", "Have you got a condom?", "I cannot control myself" and "I am a (a) homosexual, (b) lesbian".

India

When I worked on the Oxford English Dictionaries, one of the most intriguing books in our library was a battered old volume called *Hobson-Jobson*. Its full title was "Hobson-Jobson, being a glossary of Anglo-Indian colloquial words and phrases and of kindred terms, etymological, historical, geographical, and discursive – by Col. Henry Yule and the late Arthur Coke Burnell". Burnell, who worked for the Madras Civil Service, collaborated with Yule on the book before he died, and Yule published it in 1886.

In the preface, Yule described the 870-page book as a "portly double-columned edifice". It deals with words of Indian origin which have seeped into the English language. The book's title, Hobson-Jobson, is explained as a corruption of Arabic "Ya Hasan! Ya Husain!" – a cry uttered by Muslims at the Muharram festival bewailing the death of Muhammad's grandsons, Hasan and Husain. British soldiers used Hobson-Jobson to describe Indian festivals and the term came to apply to the process by which words are assimilated from foreign languages.

Yule notes that words like *calico, chintz* and *gingham* had already entered English before the reign of James I. These were all types of cloth exported from India. Calico got its name from the Indian city of Calicut, which was the first place in India that Vasco da Gama visited in 1498. Chintz, a particoloured cloth, was originally a painted or stained calico, taking its name from the plural of Hindustani *chit*, a word for a stain or spattering.

John Stockdale's book *The Indian Vocabulary* (1788) listed many words which entered the English language from Indian sources. His glossary includes *caste* or *cast*, a tribe; *chit*, a note; *loot*, plunder, pillage; *sarries*, a species of cloth; and *toddy*, the fermented juice of the date or palmyra tree.

Anglo-Indian terms proliferated from the mid-19th century when the English administered India. These naturally included words for things which the English rulers encountered in India, like dacoits, ghats, maharajahs, mahouts, monsoons, nabobs and typhoons.

Juggernaut was originally a title for Krishna, whose image was dragged through the town of Puri in Orissa on a massive cart, under whose wheels devotees flung themselves as a sacrifice. The word entered English as a term for something which ruthlessly crushes anything in its path, and hence became a common word for large lorries.

The Raj enriched English with many other terms derived or corrupted from Indian languages. For example, the one-storeyed houses in Bengal gave us the word *bungalow*, which comes from the Hindustani *bangla,* meaning "of Bengal". Outside the bungalow you might find a *veranda*, another Indian word (from Hindi *varanda*). We also borrowed *compound* to describe the area around a house or other building.

Many words which we don't necessarily associate with India actually originated there. *Shampoo* derives from Hindi *shampo*, meaning to massage.

Dinghy, from Hindi *dingi*, meant a rowing boat in India, and Brits added the H to indicate the pronunciation with a hard G. Another boat – the *catamaran* – comes from a Tamil term for a raft made of logs tied together. *Thug* was an Indian word for a cheat or swindler but came to be applied to professional killers and robbers. *Khaki* is an Urdu word meaning "dust-coloured", and the peppery soup *mulligatawny* is a corruption of Tamil *milagutannir*, meaning "pepper-water".

Much vocabulary reflects the fact that the British were the rulers in India, where they were given respectful titles like *sahib* and *memsahib*. Indian soldiers serving the British army were called *sepoys*. The Pariahs were one of the lower Indian castes, often employed as servants by the British, who came to call someone they despised a *pariah*. The British were kept cool by *punkah-wallahs*, who worked the fans. *Wallah* comes from the Hindi *–wala*, a suffix used to describe a person or thing that does something, and it was taken up by the British as a general word for a person. When entry to the Civil Service was opened to competition in 1856, people from Haileybury (the school which formerly trained entrants for the East India Company's civil service) used *competition-wallah* as a derisive term for anyone who entered the service through competition. British soldiers called army padres *amen-wallahs*.

The presence of British soldiery in India ensured the transmission of slang terms into British English. They adopted the Urdu word *kushi* (meaning pleasure) as *cushy*, describing anything easy or comfortable. The Hindi *pakka*, meaning cooked or mature, was turned into *pukka* to describe something genuine. Soldiers called mad or foolish people *doolally* (originally *doolally-tap*), after the sanatorium in the town of Deolali near Bombay. *Blighty* was their word for Britain, corrupted from Urdu *bilayati* which meant "foreign" or "European". British soldiers were aware of the dangers of the disease *cholera morbus*, which they euphemized as *Colonel Forbes*!

India continued to influence our language even when Britain began to lose its power over the sub-continent. One of the activists who undermined that power was Gandhi, whose influential teachings and methods ensured that westerners learnt such Indian terms as *ahimsa* (refusal to harm living things), *ashram* (a Sanskrit word for a hermitage or religious retreat*)*, *harijans* (Gandhi's name for "untouchables"), *sarvodaya* (the welfare of all) and *satyagraha* (non-violent action, from *satya* truth and *agraha* force*)*. And of course Gandhi was called "Mahatma", from a Sanskrit word meaning "great soul".

India as a country of spiritual enlightenment gave us the Sanskrit word *guru* for a spiritual teacher and hence for anyone dispensing wisdom. *Pundit* (from Hindi *pandit*) similarly describes a learned person. The Indian prime minister from 1947 to 1964 was widely known as Pandit Nehru. Other words associated with Indian spirituality are *darshan, karma, mantra* and *maharishi.* When jazz guitarist John McLaughlin formed a band including Indian musicians, he named it *Shakti*, a Sanskrit word for energy or power.

From the 1960s onwards, westerners like the Beatles became interested in Indian music, teaching us such terms as *raga* and *tala,* and introducing us to Indian instruments like the sitar, tabla, tambura, sarod, vina and the sarangi (a bowed instrument which produces those wailing sounds familiar from some of Satyajit Ray's films).

An Indian Glossary, compiled in 1800 by T. T. Roberts, listed *curry* as "a mixture, eaten by all the inhabitants of India". The word *curry* for a dish cooked with strong spices is actually found in English as early as the 16th century but the modern popularity of Indian food in Britain has introduced many related terms into our language.

George Whitworth's *Anglo-Indian Dictionary* (1885) included "*Chapati*, a thin flat cake; especially one of flour and water, without leaven, baked on a griddle". The OED includes such words as *pilau* and *tandoori* from as early as the 17th century. *Basmati, poppadom* and *chutney* are found in 19th-century English, while *vindaloo* occurs in W. H. Dave's 1888 book *Wife's Help to Indian Cookery.*

The word *balti* seems to have originated in Birmingham where "balti houses" proliferated in the early 1980s – cheap restaurants serving highly-spiced food in wide metal pans. The word may derive from *balti*, a Hindi word for a bucket, although there are several other possibilities, including a connection with Baltistan, a region of Kashmir.

The popularity of Indian food in Britain is just one sign of a multicultural society. So-called "Asian" people (Brits with Indian forebears) are also generating a mixture of Indian and English vocabulary known as Hinglish (from *Hindi + English*). This came to many people's attention with the TV comedy series *Goodness Gracious Me* and *The Kumars at No. 42,* which both featured Asians living in Britain. The shows parodied British attitudes towards Asians and vice versa – such as the Kapoor and Rabindranath families, who insisted that their names were anglicized to Cooper and Robinson. The shows were sprinkled with Indian slang phrases like "kiss my chuddies" (chuddies meaning underpants).

Hinglish is gaining influence in Britain because many aspects of Asian culture are fashionable. The trend probably started when Indian popular music was combined with western rock and disco music to produce *bhangra.*

Another influence has been people's increasing familiarity with Bollywood (*Bombay + Hollywood*) films.

Young people pick up Hinglish vocabulary from their Asian friends, so that we may increasingly hear such words as *haina* (a Hinglish equivalent of *innit*), *yaar* (a friend), *would-be* (someone engaged to be married*), badmash* (a hooligan or dishonest person) and *kitty party* (a gathering of women).

One particularly interesting Hinglish word is *stepney*, which originally meant a spare tyre for a vehicle (designed to be clamped over a flat tyre). It is in the OED from 1907 in this sense, and it got its name from Stepney Street in the Welsh town of Llanelli, where the spare was manufactured. But now the word is used – in Britain as well as India – for anything spare, especially as a derogatory expression for a "spare" woman or mistress.

Americanisms

We all know that Bernard Shaw said "England and America are two countries divided by a common language". Unfortunately, nobody seems to have found this quotation anywhere in Shaw's writings. Oscar Wilde echoed the sentiment when he said that "We have really everything in common with America nowadays, except, of course, language".

The phenomenon is not new. In the late 18th century, a man called Witherspoon applied the word "Americanisms" to words and constructions which differed from those used in Great Britain. Noah Webster accentuated the divide in his 1806 dictionary, where he tried to regularize spelling, starting a trend which gave American English such distinctive spellings as *ax, color, center, defense, traveled, jewelry* and *plow*. Webster's 1806 book was called *A Compendious Dictionary of the English Language* but, perhaps symptomatically, the title had changed by 1828 to *An American Dictionary of the English Language*. In 1889, Rudyard Kipling was asserting: "The American I have heard up to the present is a tongue as distinct from English as Patagonian".

We are reminded of the gulf between the UK and the USA every time we come up against the numerous differences between our two vocabularies. The American use of *gotten* still sounds strange to most Britons. Where the English tend to fill in a form, Americans tend to fill it out; when we meet somebody, they meet with somebody; when we visit someone, they visit with someone. There is a well-known range of other cases where American usage differs from ours. They often call a wallet a *billfold*, a nappy a *diaper*, a cupboard a *closet*, a tap a *faucet*, and a postcode a *zip code*. When we play noughts and crosses, they play *tic-tac-toe*; when we play draughts, they play *checkers*. They have different interpretations of such terms as *corn, vest, public school, pants* and *suspenders*. And they generally prefer *mommy* to *mummy*, *deviltry* to *devilry*, *jello* to *jelly*, *math* to *maths*, and *snicker* to *snigger*.

Yet such differences become smoothed out as we adjust ourselves to new imports. Nowadays, most of us use words like *blizzard, bogus, caucus, hamburger, lengthy, maverick, shyster* and *whistle-stop* without even realising that they probably originated in the USA. In 1997, an article by Robert McCrum in the *Observer* commented on the fact that the American popularity of "reading groups" or "book clubs" (regular meetings to discuss particular books) was starting to catch on in Britain. A few years later, we all know what they are – although in Britain they are often called "book groups". Less commendably, we have adopted the tendency of American advertisers to respell words in supposedly trendy ways: like *kool, kwik, nite* and *thru*.

It is inevitable that British English will be influenced by Americanisms, given the large number of American publications, films and television programmes that reach these shores. As long ago as 1894, Mark Twain affirmed that "There is no such thing as the Queen's English. The property has gone into the hands of a joint stock company and we own the bulk of the shares".

Even then, some expressions keep themselves to the USA and seem reluctant to cross the Atlantic. Most Britons have apparently not taken up such Americanisms as *scofflaw* (someone who flouts the law), *Buffalo wings* (deep-fried spicy chicken wings), *skidoo* (a motorized toboggan), *wingtip* (a kind of shoe), or *fall* (meaning autumn). Nor have we adopted that street sign that you see in so many American films and TV shows: reading "Don't Walk".

6

New words for old

Language change

Just as it is inevitable that English in Britain changes with influences from abroad, our language also alters to reflect changes in society. However much we may dislike these changes in usage, they occur if enough people follow them. In this way, language is a democratic process. Many people are unhappy with coinages like *accessorize* or *decluttering*, but these words entered the language – and therefore also entered dictionaries.

In fact dictionaries can serve as indicators of changes in fashion. If a new word is included in a dictionary, it is usually because that word has been taken up by enough people who find it useful to describe something new: perhaps an invention or discovery, or simply an idea or concept that has become popular. The big *Oxford English Dictionary* is a useful tool in tracking these developments, because it tries to find the earliest printed example of every word.

For example, the differences between young and old people became so evident in the 1960s that the phrase *generation gap* entered the language around 1962. This change was anticipated as early as 1941 by the American coinage *teenager*, which described a type of person who had not previously been categorized. The 1950s saw the new craze for *rock and roll* (or *rock 'n' roll*), which marked a growing gap between young and old – who had previously enjoyed the same types of music. Youthful rebellion was also signposted around that time by such 1954 coinages as *blackboard jungle* (from the title of a book by Evan Hunter), *student politics* and *Teddy boy*.

One area notable for rapid language change is the fashion world, where what is fashionable this year may be passé next year. They may have been the height of fashion in their time but words like *Crimplene, Day-Glo, hot pants, legwarmer* and *tank top* have clearly passed their sell-by date.

The effect of social change on language is illustrated by this list of words that (according to the *OED*) entered the language in the years between 1950 and 2000. They describe new inventions and concepts as well as some of the concerns which were uppermost in people's minds during those years. The list provides a snapshot of social history:

1950 zebra crossing

1951 blast-off

1952 action painting

1953 CinemaScope

1954 data processing

1955 subtopia, track suit

1956 brinkmanship

1957 consenting adult, Viet Cong

1958 hula hoop, thalidomide

1959 traffic warden

1960 breathalyser, Velcro

1961 bionic

1962 fish finger

1963 Beatlemania

1964 skateboard

1965 metrication, silicon chip

1966 kung-fu

1967 encounter group, phone-in

1968 unisex

1969 bovver boot

1970 doomwatch

1971 chairperson

1972 real ale

1973 streaker (naked runner)

1974 leg warmer, teletext

1975 Sloane Ranger

1976 Bollywood

1977 step-parenting

1978 job-share (as a verb), me-ism, telephone banking

1979 compact disc, Space Invaders

1980 air guitar, petrolhead

1981 paparazzi, wannabe

1982 Argie, break-dancing, email

1983 video nasty

1984 yuppie

1985 annus horribilis, gobsmacked

1986 multitask (as a verb)

1987 greenwash, ram raid (as a noun)

1988 e-book, luvvie, road rage

1989 B-lister, C-lister (minor celebrities), macchiato

1990 emoticon, World Wide Web

1991 carjacking, ethnic cleansing

1992 e-business, shedload

1993 weblog

1994 dotcom

1995 ladette, webcam

1996 gastropub, Viagra

1997 Tamagotchi

1998 Bluetooth, chav

1999 bling, blog

2000 Sudoku

These words and phrases seem to encapsulate the mood of a particular moment but some expressions were coined at unexpected times. For example, you might expect *acid rain* to have entered the language in recent years, when people became more concerned about the environment, but the phrase was first used in 1845. If you thought that double-glazing salesmen are a very modern nuisance, the OED has found *double-glazing* from 1943 but, amazingly enough, *double-glazed* was in use in 1910. *Spaceship* dates from 1880; *contact lens* is found as early as 1888; and *feminist* is found in 1894.

Quiz 3

To test your awareness of language, try to guess the first date (within, say, ten years) given in the OED (2nd edition, 1989) for these expressions. Some of the answers may surprise you!
1. sauna. 2. cash dispenser. 3. mustard gas. 4. homosexual (adjective). 5. modern art. 6. bird watching. 7. launderette. 8. videocassette. 9. escalator. 10. shorthand typist.

Coinages

The English language probably contains at least half a million words. Each one of these words must, at some time or other, have been uttered for the very first time. Occasionally it is easy to discover who first used a word. For instance, the word *ageism* was coined in 1969 by Dr Robert Butler, an

American specialist in geriatric medicine. American basketball player Derek Smith claims that he invented the phrase *high-five* in 1979 to describe the celebratory gesture of people slapping their right hands together over their heads. Earlier coinages include Edmund Spenser's *blatant*, John Milton's *pandemonium*, Jonathan Swift's *Lilliputian*, Horace Walpole's *serendipity*, Jeremy Bentham's *international*, T. H. Huxley's *agnostic* and Joseph Heller's *catch-22*.

Of course, one of the most prolific inventors of words was Shakespeare, who apparently introduced such words as *aerial, assassination, bare-faced, countless, critic* and *critical, disgraceful, eventful, exposure, lack-lustre, laughable, militarist, monumental* and *savagery* as well as phrases like *foregone conclusion, on purpose, salad days,* and *the seamy side.* Shakespeare also expanded the language by his use of metaphorical phrases – like *breathing your last, cudgelling your brain,* and *wearing your heart on your sleeve.* He also made words serve as new parts of speech – like *backward* in "the dark backward and abysm of time".

The *Oxford English Dictionary* sets itself the daunting task of tracing the first use of every word, but this is not always possible. Often the best the OED can do is to record the first use of a word that they have found in print. And new words are being created constantly – a conservative estimate suggests that at least three new words enter the language every day. This means that dictionaries have difficulties keeping up. In *The King's English*, H. W. Fowler pointed out that *appendicitis* was omitted from the first edition of the OED, because it came into the language after the appropriate volume was published in 1885.

New words and phrases are called neologisms. In its early use, neologism was generally a pejorative term: implying that the new word was an unwanted upstart. Gradually even the purists began to accept that new words were needed for new concepts and inventions. Technology continually supplies us with new devices which require new names. So the first decade of the 20th century brought us such words as *airliner, bakelite, conveyor belt, escalator, lie-detector, Meccano, radio* and *television,* as well as *jazz, Oxford marmalade* (registered as a trade-mark by Frank Cooper in 1908), *pacifism, peanut butter, pineapple chunks, Rottweilers* and *suffragettes.* The 1990s gave us *Aga saga, crop circle, cybercafé, docusoap, DVD, Gulf War syndrome,* and *speed camera.*

When a neologism becomes fashionable, it often leads to imitations. The phenomenon of the *sit-in* gave rise to the *love-in* and the *be-in,* while *Watergate* has spawned numerous other words ending in *–gate* for scandals of various kinds. When people started to talk and write about weapons of mass destruction (or WMD), we soon encountered imitative phrases like weapons of mass deception, weapons of mass distortion, and weapons of mass hysteria.

Some new words fall out of the language almost as quickly as they come in. In 1996 people started worrying about the *millennium bug*; now the phrase sounds as outdated as the Millennium Dome. Also in the 1990s, the popularity of the Spice Girls led to much talk about *girl power*: another phrase which now sounds old-fashioned.

On the other hand, many words survive in the language which aroused criticism when they first appeared. Edward Phillips's *New World of Words* (1678) deprecated as "affected" and even "barbarous, and illegally compounded" such new words as *agonize, autograph, bibliography, ferocious, misogynist* and *repatriation*. H. W. Fowler noted that the *Spectator* in 1905 apologised for using the "convenient neologism" *intellectuals* (even though the OED has examples from 1652 onwards). Fowler himself disliked the word *racial*, which he called "an ugly word, the strangeness of which is due to our instinctive feeling that the termination *–al* has no business at the end of a word that is not obviously Latin".

Needed words

We have looked at the ways that new words get into the language. But what can you do if English doesn't include a word with a meaning you want to express? You may have to make up a new word yourself. In 2004, two BBC radio programmes – *Word of Mouth* on Radio 4 and *The Verb* on Radio 3 – ran competitions to find new words that we need in the language. Listeners' suggestions were sometimes frivolous, like *testoblerone*, a hormone to give you the strength to break a Swiss chocolate bar. Several of the entries were blends like this: fusing two words together, as in *pigmatic* (pig-headed and dogmatic) or *windswiper* (windscreen wiper).

The *Word of Mouth* contest was won by another blend: *sprognosis*, the science of determining the sex of a baby. The runners-up included *festilities*, the gathering together of relatives who don't get on with one another, and *diagony*, frustration experienced behind someone zig-zagging about. Other suggestions included *stailer*, a TV trailer that is repeated over and over again, and *studentile*, regressive behaviour like pushing your friends around in supermarket trolleys. And listeners suggested ways of pronouncing that awkward "www" in website addresses: either "treble-yew", "sextupleyew" or "wee-wee-wee". One listener reported that in New Zealand they say "dub-

dub-dub". Entries in *The Verb*'s competition included *ginspiration* (meaning a brainwave) and *verbiform*, to make up new words.

One of the words most needed in English is a pronoun that can refer indiscriminately to a male or female. A pedantic caller to a local radio programme complained that, if you dial 1471 to find out who has phoned you recently, British Telecom's stock of responses includes "The caller withheld their number". The pedant complained that this should be "his or her number" – although this sounds rather awkward – or that BT should have changed the message to something like "The caller's number has been withheld" (although this doesn't explain whether it was the caller or BT that withheld the number).

Strictly speaking, our pedant was correct: a singular pronoun should follow a singular subject – although one might ask what you should do in a case like "A handful of bathers was (or were?) swimming in the sea". Here the singular noun *handful* would normally require "was" but "were" probably sounds more natural because it is preceded by the plural "bathers". Our language really needs a sexless word for these occasions – and plenty of suggestions have been made, including *sie, sim, zie, zir, e, em, hir, hisher* and *shimself* – but none of these has caught on. Perhaps we should just accept *their* and the like; after all, Fowler points out that the *OED* quotes examples by Goldsmith, Thackeray, Bagehot ("Nobody in their senses") and Bernard Shaw.

An article in *New Scientist* discussed the problems associated with plastic bags, which are now widely used by shoppers but which can become a problem when they are thrown away. The Marine Conservation Society's director of conservation solemnly explained: "Plastic bags exceed what you would anticipate would be their pollution impact, because they're so much more mobile than other types of litter". So you see plastic bags blowing around the streets or flapping in the branches of trees. This new phenomenon clearly needs a name. In Ireland they are called *witches' knickers*; in South Africa *the national flower*; and in China *white pollution*. Other names include *plastic snow, Hackney roses* and (in the USA) *Arkansas tumbleweeds* or *Jersey tumbleweeds*.

A regular column in the *Atlantic Monthly* discusses "word fugitives" – words that are not in the language but should be, because they are wanted to describe common happenings. For example, how would you describe the tendency to believe there is significance in two events occurring simultaneously, even though there is no evidence to link them together? Suggestions included *fauxincidence, duperstition, coincivince* and *wishful linking*.

English also lacks a word for the familiar observation that, when you are standing in a queue, other queues seem to move faster than yours. We also need a word to describe the fact that your symptoms disappear as soon as you get to see the doctor, or the occasion when a technical device that you thought was broken suddenly starts working when a repairer simply looks at it. I quite like the phrase *devious ex machina* to describe this last event.

Gelett Burgess invented the word *blurb* to describe the eulogistic description of a book, usually printed on its cover or flyleaf. He probably had no idea that it would catch on, and become a respectable English word. The same thing occurred when the author Horace Walpole in 1754 coined *serendipity*, which was taken up eagerly by people wanting to describe the faculty for accidentally discovering useful things. I wish the same had happened to H. L. Mencken's coinage *ombibulous*, aptly describing someone who drinks anything.

In *The Meaning of Liff* (1983), Douglas Adams and John Lloyd invented many new but necessary words by adapting place-names. For example, they say that an *Amersham* is a sneeze which tickles but never comes (a phenomenon which someone else christened *antishoopation*). *Symond's Yat* is the little spoonful inside the lid of a recently opened boiled egg. An *Esher* is a tap that squirts out too much water, causing a *Botley* or water stain on the crotch of your trousers. A similar trouser stain is a *Piddletrenthide*.

Rich Hall and some of his friends wrote a book called *Sniglets* (1987) which devises words that don't exist but ought to. Their coinages are not very inventive but they come up with some senses that certainly need words: like *beavo* (a pencil with teeth marks all over it), *flurrant* (the one leaf that always clings to the end of a rake) and *yaffling* (speaking loudly to foreigners as if, somehow, this makes you easier to understand).

Dictionaries are full of words that have fallen out of use but might well be revived. The *Shorter Oxford Dictionary* includes such unfairly neglected items as *bangster* (a bully or ruffian), *belly-timber* (a dialect word for food or provisions), *eye-service* (the doing of work only when watched by an employer or master), *flesh-quake* (a trembling of the body), *merry-go-down* (strong ale), *natiform* (resembling or having the form of buttocks), *poplolly* (a mistress) and *smellfungus* (a grumbler or fault-finder). I am particularly intrigued by *grimthorpe*, which means "to restore an ancient building with lavish expenditure rather than skill or taste" – derived from the name of Lord Grimthorpe, "whose restoration of St Albans Cathedral, completed in 1904, aroused fierce criticism and controversy".

Some words are known to logophiles as overspecialized words, because they have such specialized meanings that it is hard to imagine situations where you would need to use them. I assembled some of these overspecialized words for a quiz in my book *Oxford Word Challenge*, including *alerion* (an eagle without beak or feet), *chiliomb* (a sacrifice of a thousand oxen) and *paneity* (the quality or condition of being bread). Some of these words have such mysterious meanings as to make them virtually unusable. They include *ambilevous* (left-handed on both sides), *amphisbaenous* (walking equally in opposite directions), *anemocracy* (a government by the wind) and *shrew-struck* (paralysed as the result of being overrun by a shrew-mouse).

Divination seems to have given rise to several such words, like *lecanomancy*, which means divination by inspecting water in a basin, *ornithomancy*, divination by means of the flight and cries of birds, and *scapulimancy* – divination by means of the cracks in a burned shoulder-blade bone.

Perhaps there is still a use for words like *vexillology* (the study of flags), *serein* (a fine rain falling in tropical climates from a cloudless sky) and *haecceity* (the quality of a thing that makes it unique or describable as "this (one)"). And if you live next door to the neighbour from hell, you may find it useful to know about *stillicidium*, which is "(a right or duty relating to) the drainage of rainwater from the eaves of a building on to another's property".

Words of the year

When a year ends, it has become customary for awards to be given out for achievements in various fields, especially entertainment, and we are inundated with awards ceremonies.

Nowadays, awards are even given to words – and several organisations choose a "Word of the Year". This can be the word that most aptly typifies what has happened that year. That was certainly the case when the American Dialect Society chose *subprime* as Word of the Year for 2007 – a word which will live in infamy. The financial crisis partly caused by subprime mortgages was reflected by the ADS choosing *bailout* as its Word of the Year for 2008.

Other words favoured in 2007 by the American Dialect Society included the useful *wrap-rage* (anger caused by trying to open a tightly-sealed item) and *quadriboobage* (appearing to have four breasts when a woman wears a brassiére which is too small).

Also in 2007, the Australian *Macquarie Dictionary* chose *pod-slurping* (downloading large amounts of data from a computer) as its Word of the Year, although its readers' favourite coinage was *password fatigue* (weariness caused by having too many passwords on your computer to remember).

Computers likewise figured in Macquarie's list of suggested buzz-words for 2008. So *dub-a-dub-dub* is a spoken form of www – the prefix for website addresses, and *Wii shoulder* is an ailment brought about by playing virtual computer games. One frightening novelty is *PODS*: a method of controlling parking with a device underneath a parking bay which tells a traffic warden when a car has exceeded the time limit (it stands for Parking Overstay Detection System). Macquarie's ultimate choice for 2008's Word of the Year was *toxic debt*.

The Macquarie list also showed how much environmental concerns have affected the language, with coinages like *water footprint* for the amount of fresh water used by a person, business or country. *Climate porn* is a handy phrase for exaggerated predictions about global warming.

Other choices for Word of the Year reflect current social trends. Our modern concern with obesity is mirrored in Macquarie's Word of the Year from 2006: *muffin top*, a fold of fat which protrudes over the top of trousers or skirts on an overweight woman.

In the same year, the American Dialect Society chose *Plutoed* – meaning devalued or demoted, as happened to the former planet Pluto when it was no longer deemed to be a planet. More long-lasting were other nominated words like *waterboarding* (a form of torture).

Many new words are created by blending together two existing words. Recent coinages of this sort include *frenemy* (an enemy who falsely pretends to your friend); *bromance* (an intense but non-sexual friendship between two men); *jargonaut* (someone who uses lots of jargon); *chillax* (chill out and relax); and *cyberchondriac* (a hypochondriac who gets information from the internet).

Blending was one of the main devices used by the mischievous Charlie Brooker in his own list of invented words in the *Guardian*. For example, he defined *auntiepathy* as "ingrained tabloid hostility towards the BBC", and *plebbledash* as "to bulk up a television news report with needless vox-pop soundbites from ill-informed members of the public".

One word which has deservedly been resuscitated is *bankster* – a mixture of banker and gangster. This encapsulation of some bankers' unreliability was apparently coined by *Time* magazine in the 1930s – the time of the Great Depression. It seemed to have fallen into disuse but it has been revived in recent years as many people became sceptical about bankers.

Modern cynicism is also typified by the word *meh*, which came top of the list when *Collins English Dictionary* asked the public to suggest words to include in the next edition. *Meh* is an interjection or adjective indicating boredom or a lack of interest.

A survey by the OUP of new words and phrases suggested that *footprint* (as in *carbon footprint*) is one of the words most typical of the 21st century, although people who voted in the survey decided that the prevalent word for our century was actually a date: *9/11*.

Back-formations

Many new words are formed by adding letters at the beginning or end of other words. Thus we get *catlike* by adding the suffix *-like* to *cat*, and *unsuitable* is formed by adding the prefix *un-* to *suitable*. More complex changes are involved when a word like *beauty* gives birth to *beautiful, beauteous, beautician* and *beautify*, but it is still a process of something being added to an existing word.

However, new words can be created by removing some of the letters from an existing word. *Advertisement* becomes shortened to *advert* and then *ad*, while *flu* is created by removing some letters from the beginning and end of *influenza*. A special category of this process is called back-formation, when a prefix or suffix seems to have been removed from a word, usually to make a different part of speech. So the noun *choreography* is clipped to turn it into the verb *choreograph*, and the adjective *aesthetic* gives us the back-formation *aesthete*.

Although back-formations are widespread in English, a few pedants dislike them. This may be because some back-formations sound awkward when we first hear them. How do you react to a sightseer becoming someone who *sightsees*, or attrition leading to the verb *attrit*, or enthusiasm creating the verb *enthuse*?

In the late 1960s, 76 per cent of a usage panel found *enthuse* unacceptable. As recently as 1997, 65 per cent of the panel voted against it. The *Oxford English Dictionary* calls enthuse "an ignorant back-formation from enthusiasm" but it has plenty of quotations to show that the word is well-established – both as a transitive verb (to make enthusiastic) and an intransitive verb (to be enthusiastic). And *sight-see* is found as a verb in 1824 – the same date as *sight-seeing*.

In fact back-formations like these are a common phenomenon in English. Probably the most numerous cases are where a noun is changed into a verb, like the aforemetioned *choreograph* and *enthuse*. There are plenty of others, such as *babysit* (from *babysitter*), *resurrect* (from *resurrection*) and *televise* (from *television*). Some of these back-formations may strike you as strange, like the verbs *problem-solve* and *price-fix*, but the OED has convincing evidence of their existence.

The words for people who have specific jobs or pastimes often give birth to verbs which describe what they do. A housekeeper housekeeps, a burglar burgles, a plumber plumbs, a commuter commutes, a butler buttles and an usher ushes.

Nouns can easily be formed from adjectives, like *raunch* from *raunchy* and *sleaze* from *sleazy*. Many words ending in -ing give rise to back-formations. So we get the verb *to brainwash* from *brainwashing*, and *to fine-tune* from *fine tuning*. After the famous relief of Mafeking in 1900, people soon coined the verb *maffick*, meaning to celebrate

Some back-formations might justifiably be described as "ignorant" or "unacceptable" because they arise from misunderstandings. In 1926, Fowler's *Modern English Usage* pointed out that the verb to *scavenge* is a back-formation from scavenger, but "the normal verb [is} to *scavenger*". *Pease* was originally a singular word but people mistakenly took it for a plural and created *pea* as a new singular which has replaced *pease* except in such combinations as *pease pudding*. *Assets* also started life as a singular noun (from the Anglo-French phrase *aver assetz*, to have enough) but it was soon regarded as a plural, so that something could be an asset.

The earliest use of the noun *ware* was to denote things manufactured or made for selling. Hence it was tacked onto all kinds of words, as in *ironware*, *tableware* and (named after my home town) *Tunbridge ware*. With the arrival of computers, *hardware* and *software* took on new meanings and the suffix *-ware* was revived as a kind of back-formation, creating such constructions as *courseware* and *shareware*. *Vapourware* is apparently techno-speak for a marvellous technological device which is announced but never materializes.

If you ever go into a burger bar and order a burger, remember that it is a back-formation from *hamburger*, and has spawned such variants as *beefburger*, *cheeseburger, eggburger* and *steakburger*. In her 1982 book *Having It All*, the American author Helen Gurley Brown coined the word *mouseburger* for a shy or timid woman.

Obsolesence

Dictionaries get bigger and bigger. This is inevitable, since most dictionaries have to find space for new words entering the language (perhaps more than three per day), while it is hard to decide if any words deserve to be deleted.

Choosing which new words to add to a dictionary is comparatively easy. So long as you have enough evidence of their use, you can insert them. When

I worked on the Oxford Dictionaries, a rule of thumb was that you had to find a word used five times in printed sources for it to be worth including.

It is much harder to judge if a word can be removed from a dictionary because it is no longer being used. The only evidence of a word being obsolete is often negative: you can't find evidence for it, but someone somewhere might still be using it.

A while ago, the Editor of *Collins English Dictionary* said he intended to delete 24 words from his dictionary to make space for more inclusions. It was a rather obvious publicity stunt, because he said he needed to make space to add 2,000 new words! Nonetheless, he was willing to consider leaving in any of the 24 obsolete words if their deletion was convincingly challenged.

Thereupon various celebrities championed old words in the list. Andrew Motion wanted to keep *skirr* (a whirring sound), while Stephen Fry chose *fubsy* (short and stout).

Other words on the threatened list included *agrestic, embrangle, fatidical, oppugnant* and *vilipend*. Yet how can the Collins people be sure that these words are never used?

Andrew Motion claimed that *skirr* is still used by birdwatchers to describe the fluttering of birds' wings. The *OED*'s latest quotation for the word is 1887 but it lists two occurrences in novels by Thomas Hardy, so readers are still likely to come across the word and wonder what it means.

Perhaps the Collins people should have been more scrupulous and consulted the *OED*, which includes recent quotations for several words on the Collins list, such as *malison* (a curse – 1991), *mansuetude* (kindness – 1993), *muliebrity* (womanliness – 1997), *niddering* (cowardly – 1999) and *olid* (smelling foul – 2001).

It is easy to see if some types of words are obsolete – especially when the thing they referred to has ceased to exist. A *dandiprat* used to be a small coin (worth three halfpennies) but it would now only be used historically, although its transferred sense "an urchin" may still be familiar from its use in Malcolm Arnold's overture *Beckus the Dandipratt*.

Other coins like farthings, florins, angels and testoons have also gone out of use. Farthings were no longer legal tender after 1961, but the word may still crop up in sayings like "not worth a brass farthing".

Some words become obsolete fairly quickly, because they are fashionable only for a short time. The *Concise Oxford Dictionary*'s tenth edition removed *cowabunga* (an exclamation of delight popularized in the 1960s by the Teenage Mutant Ninja Turtles) and *cassingle* (an audio cassette with one tune on each side).

Other words that date quite quickly are swear words, since new ones come along remarkably quickly to replace those that sound out-of-date – like *gadzooks, zounds, forsooth* and *egad.*

Some words definitely sound archaic and have therefore dropped out of use except in historical contexts. These are words like *alack, avaunt, lackaday, prithee, thee* and *thou*. Yet we still recognize them, often because they are used in such familiar sources as Shakespeare and the Bible.

The Pilgrim Fathers were certainly familiar with the Bible (and probably Shakespeare) when they emigrated to America in the early 17th century. Because they lived fairly sheltered lives, their successors held on to various expressions which became obsolete in Britain, although they could still be found in various English dialects. So the Americans went on using such words as *bub* (=boy), *fall* (meaning autumn), *muss* (a disturbance or dispute), *beef* (meaning a cow or ox), *catty-cornered* (diagonal), *pesky, chomp* and *julep.* Some of these words have come back into mainstream British English – virtually borrowed back from the Americans.

The continuous expansion of English means that new editions of dictionaries will grow in size. Of course, they can save space by shortening or even omitting definitions for words which are so common that people will hardly ever look them up. Yet English dictionaries for foreign learners will still need entries for common words like *dog* and *cat*, as well as explanations of our strange uses of such words as *get* and *put.*

However, some lexicographers are notorious for either being long-winded or for including their personal prejudices in definitions. Thomas Blount's *Glossographia* (1656) defined *honeymoon* as "applied to those married persons that love well at first and decline in affection afterwards. It is hony now, but it will change as the moon".

Personal prejudice obtruded into the *Oxford English Dictionary Supplement* (1976) when the Editor, R. W. Burchfield, described *insinuendo* (a blend of *insinuation* and *innuendo*) as "A tasteless word", even though there were five illustrative quotations, including one from Compton Mackenzie.

Rarities

Should words be deleted from a dictionary because they are obsolete? The *Oxford English Dictionary* apparently labels 87,458 words as "Obs", which may seem a lot until you remember that the *OED* covers more than half a million words and combinations.

You can understand why some words have become obsolete: like *bumdockdousse*, which the *OED* defines as "Urquhart's word for *pimpompet*, 'a kinde of game wherein three hit each other on the bumme with one of their feet'". And there are fewer chances nowadays to use the word *bungie-bird*: "a contemptuous designation for a (?Franciscan) friar".

The decrease in superstition may also have led to many words for phobias becoming obsolete. Fewer people seem to be plagued by *batrachophobia* (dread of frogs, toads, newts, etc.), although the *OED* suggests that many people still have *triskaidekaphobia* (fear of the number thirteen). And those of us who hate people cycling on pavements might take heart from the fact that the *Westminster Gazette* reported in 1896 that "The cycling craze has produced the antagonistic disease of cyclophobia".

Some people enjoy bursting the bubbles in bubble-wrap, but our language appears to lack a word for those devoted to this practice. Perhaps we could revive *utricide*, which the *OED* defines as "one who stabs an inflated vessel of skin". And there is surely still the need for an obsolete word like *emunction* ("the action of wiping the nose").

The *OED*'s only evidence for the word *contubernial* is from Chaucer, but campers could surely find it valuable, as it means "sharing the same tent". Do gardeners no longer need a word like *ablaqueation*: "the breaking up or removal of the soil around the roots of trees"? And in these permissive days, there might still be a use for *wittol*, which signifies "a man who is aware of and complaisant about the infidelity of his wife; a contented cuckold".

After all, Ambrose Bierce's *Devil's Dictionary* defined *obsolete* as "No longer used by the timid. Said chiefly of words. A word which some lexicographer has marked obsolete is ever thereafter an object of dread and loathing to the fool writer, but if it is a good word and has no exact modern equivalent equally good, it is good enough for the good writer".

The *OED* doesn't label some words "Obs" even though it could find only a single occurrence of them in print. These include *dactylonomy* (the art of counting on the fingers), *epalpebrate* (having no eyebrows) and *fenestriform* (window-shaped).

The village of Saverne in Alsace became briefly famous in 1912 "when an excited German subaltern cut down a lame cobbler who smiled at him". The incident gave rise to *Zabernism* and *Zabernize* (from Zabern, the German name of the village) for the misuse of military authority, but the word apparently only lasted until 1921.

For about the same period, *Bradbury* was used in Britain as a colloquial term for a one-pound note, named after John Bradbury, Secretary to the Treasury from 1913 to 1919. Pound notes were subsequently nicknamed *Fishers*, after Bradbury's successor, Sir Warren Fisher.

Before he became president of the USA, Herbert Hoover was appointed Food Commissioner during the First World War. His encouragement of frugality led to the verb *Hooverize* being used for a short time, meaning "To be sparing or economical, especially with food". A 1918 Valentine card included the verse:

> I can Hooverize on dinner,
>
> And on lights and fuel too.
>
> But I'll never learn to Hooverize
>
> When it comes to loving you.

The word now looks like being revived in the different sense of consuming or removing something, just as a Hoover vacuum cleaner does.

As noted above, Shakespeare is credited with contributing many new expressions to the language, from *amazement* to *worthless*. But he also coined numerous words and phrases which never caught on, or fell out of the language.

Shakespeare appears to have been alone in using such expressions as *bacon-fed* (for rustic or clownish), *over-red* (to cover with blood) and *overstink* (to stink more than something else). My favourite occurs in *The Winter's Tale*, where the jealous Leontes accuses his wife of being a *bed-swerver* (an adulterer).

7

Phrases

Clichés

A jocular piece of advice tells us that we should "avoid clichés like the plague". Of course, the joke here is that avoiding something like the plague is itself a cliché – a saying that has been used so often that it is over-familiar. A longer definition is supplied by Anton Zijderveld (of the University of Tilburg in the Netherlands) in his snappily-titled *On Clichés: The Supersedure of Meaning by Function in Modernity*: "A cliché is a traditional form of human expression (in words, thoughts, emotions, gestures, acts) which – due to repetitive use in social life – has lost its original, often ingenious heuristic power".

The lexicographer Eric Partridge noted that there are several kinds of cliché: the fly-blown phrase (e.g. much of a muchness), metaphors that are now pointless (lock, stock and barrel), formulas that have become mere counters (far be it from me to…), sobriquets that have lost all their freshness (The Iron Duke), quotations that are nauseating (cups that cheer but not inebriate) and foreign phrases (*bête noire*). Clichés can also be proverbs (there's no place like home) and catchphrases (here's one I made earlier; keep on truckin').

It is notable that, when he was describing clichés, Partridge fell into employing them himself. In his *Usage and Abusage* he said "A cliché is an outworn commonplace; a phrase (or virtual phrase) that has become so hackneyed that scrupulous speakers and writers shrink from it because they feel that its use is an insult to the intelligence". And in his *Dictionary of Clichés*, he says of the cliché: "It is a phrase 'on tap', as it were". Despite his disapproval of clichés, Partridge could not avoid using clichéd phrases like "insult to the intelligence", "on tap" and "as it were".

Clichés tend to be used when people are in a hurry, or so unimaginative that they cannot think of anything better, or just lazy. Back in the 16th century, Montaigne wrote "It is always easier to draw on the storehouse of memory than to find something original to say".

Most of us fall into using clichés from time to time, especially when we want to say something to be sociable. So, if we meet someone walking in the rain, we might comment "Nice weather for ducks" and if we see someone on their way to church, we may exhort them "Say one for me". Tony Hancock, using scripts written by Galton & Simpson, often resorted to clichés, as he did at the reunion he held for his old army pals, when all they could they could think of saying were things like "A lot of water's flowed under the bridge since then" and "Nice little place you've got here".

Clichés are stereotyped phrases – and, indeed, the word cliché comes from a French term used by printers for a printing plate or stereotype used to print the same thing over and over again. Sir Ernest Gowers, in his revised version of Fowler's *Modern English Usage*, noted that "There are thousands for whom the only sound sleep is the sleep of the just; the light at dusk must always be dim, religious; all beliefs are cherished, all confidence is implicit, all ignorance blissful, all isolation splendid, all uncertainty glorious, all voids aching". George Orwell echoed these sentiments in his *Politics and the English Language*: "Prose consists less and less of words chosen for the sake of their meaning, and more and more of phrases tacked together like the sections of a prefabricated hen-house". George Baker called the cliché "a coin so battered by use as to be defaced".

These writers express the widespread view that clichés are undesirable. Winston Churchill famously upbraided Anthony Eden: "As far as I can see you have used every cliché except 'God is Love' and 'Please adjust your dress before leaving'". Ernest Bevin supposedly denounced Aneurin Bevan because "All 'e ever says is clitch, clitch, clitch, clitch".

Nevertheless, Christopher Ricks defended clichés, saying "The deliberate and responsible use of cliché can foster critical self-consciousness". James Rogers also came to the defence: "Clichés can serve as the lubricant of language: summing up a point or a situation, easing a transition in thought, adding a seasoning of humour to a discourse".

Yet most people would think the only way that a cliché can be humorous is when it is parodied, as when a sports reporter said that some football fans supported their team "through thin and thin". P. G. Wodehouse excelled at parodying clichés, as in this extract from *Sticky Wicket at Blandings*: "It was a beautiful afternoon. The sky was blue, the sun yellow, butterflies flitted, birds tooted, bees buzzed and, to cut a long story short, all Nature smiled".

Where do clichés come from? Mostly they originate as pithy phrases which somehow appeal to people's imagination, although this very appeal leads to them being overused. The BBC radio programme *Desert Island Discs* has long cited the Bible and Shakespeare as essential writings, and both are prolific sources of clichés. The Bible gives us: holy of holies, killing the fatted calf, powers that be, still small voice, and hiding your light under a bushel. Shakespeare provided us with: foregone conclusion, cudgel one's brains, breathe one's last, the bare bodkin, and to be or not to be. A naïve lady at a performance of *Hamlet* reportedly complained that the play was full of quotations. Later writers have given us: confusion worse confounded (Milton), almighty dollar (Washington Irving), big stick (Theodore Roosevelt), and the opera ain't over 'til the fat lady sings (Dan Cook).

Sports commentators like Dan Cook are notorious for using clichés, asserting that "it's a game of two halves" and "they think it's all over", while describing the players as either "sick as a parrot" or "over the moon". But clichés are equally widespread among businessmen, journalists and politicians. When the Plain English Campaign surveyed the clichés that people hate most, the list was topped by "At the end of the day" and "At this moment in time". The list also included those notoriously dishonest statements "With all due respect" and "I hear what you are saying".

Clichés can be single words, like the currently fashionable "solutions" which *Private Eye* has collected assiduously for some while (e.g. "Siemens Transportation: Efficient Rail Solutions"). An assessment of the vocabulary most frequently used on the internet came up with words like *marketplace, sustainable, teamwork, footprint* and *nuanced*, alongside such phrases as support services, state of the art, cutting edge, bottom line, mission statement and road map.

These new clichés take the place of many that have had the decency to die out. In his *Modern English Usage*, H. W. Fowler (who picturesquely calls clichés "battered ornaments") lists outdated phrases like: curses not loud but deep, have one's quiver full, and get no forrader. Jonathan Swift used many obsolete clichés in his *Complete Collection of Genteel and Ingenious Conversation* (1738), a *tour-de-force* consisting of lengthy conversations packed with trite phrases. Hackneyed expressions in Swift's day apparently included: I'm sure the gallows groans for you, some are wise and some are otherwise, and if things do not break or wear out, how should tradesmen live? However, many of the phrases listed by Swift are still known today, such as: enough's as good as a feast, talk of the devil, you can't see the wood for the trees, and I'm as old as my tongue and a little older than my teeth. When Swift's talkers prepare for bed, one of them says "I'm going to the Land of Nod" and another adds "Faith, I'm for Bedfordshire".

More than a century later, Flaubert assembled a similar collection of clichés and hackneyed ideas in his *Dictionnaire des Idées Reçues*, translated in 1954 by Jacques Barzun as *Dictionary of Accepted Ideas*. As a child, Flaubert used to note down inane things said by an old woman who visited his parents, and he came to hate banal expressions which are uttered without much thought. His dictionary includes: *accident,* always "regrettable" or "unlucky" – as if a mishap might sometimes be a cause for rejoicing; *ladies,* always come first: "God bless them!"; *restaurant,* you should order the dishes not usually served at home; when uncertain, look at what others around you are eating; *sneeze,* after saying "God bless you!" start discussing the origin of this custom; and *strong,* as a horse, an ox, a Turk, Hercules.

The most overworked clichés are catchphrases – sayings that "catch on" with the public and are then repeated *ad nauseam*. Catchphrases are commonly generated in advertisements (Drinka pinta milka day; Vorsprung durch Technik) and in comedy shows on radio and television. Indeed, on BBC Television, *The Fast Show* made a point of including as many catchphrases as it could, from "Suits you, sir" to "Where's my washboard?" Other phrases given to us by TV include "Am I bothered?" and "The only gay in the village".

The catchphrases you know and quote often suggest how old you are. People who lived through the Second World War will still remember "I don't mind if I do" and "Can you hear me, mother?", while later generations will come up with "Don't mention the war" and "This parrot is an ex-parrot". Most catchphrases have a limited life, but some remain in use for many years – like "I'll have your guts for garters", which Eric Partridge traced back to 1598.

Idioms

The *Concise Oxford Dictionary* defines a dictionary as "A book that lists the words of a language in alphabetical order and gives their meaning, or their equivalent in a different language". However, I have become increasingly aware of the limitations of dictionaries because they concentrate on words rather than clusters of words.

This concentration was evident right from the start of the Oxford dictionaries, when James Murray issued his appeal in 1879 for readers willing to peruse books in search of items for inclusion in a new dictionary.

Murray instructed them to "Make a quotation for every word that strikes you as rare, obsolete, old-fashioned, new, peculiar or used in a particular way". Note how Murray was implying that he wanted readers to collect words, not combinations or phrases. Of course, these also found their way into the *Oxford English Dictionary* and its various spin-offs, but the emphasis on single words meant that these books have tended to underrate other linguistic elements.

Dictionaries accustom us to the idea that language consists of individual words, but language is often put together in chunks: prefabricated beams and sections as well as separate bricks. When we speak or write, we don't just use words: we employ a whole range of phrases, including clichés, allusions, proverbs, metaphors, similes, quotations – and especially idioms.

Idioms can be defined as phrases whose meaning cannot be inferred from the senses of the separate words. Idioms don't mean what they (seem to) say. One learned writer defined idioms as "Conventionalized multiword expressions, often but not always non-literal". Yet we seldom stop to ponder what idioms are – we take them for granted – in the same way that many lexicographers have taken them for granted. Incidentally, the *Concise Oxford Dictionary* includes "take something for granted" but seems to omit such idioms as *take a back seat, take someone as you find him, take effect* and *take some beating.* We use idioms without much thought because they encapsulate ideas concisely, effectively and often vividly. So we say "Make yourself at home" instead of "Have as much freedom, comfort, etc. as you would if you were in your own home".

Many idioms trip easily off the tongue because they are alliterative: like *might and main, rack and ruin, chop and change, tit for tat, day by day, hither and thither, spick and span, kith and kin.* The last two of these examples illustrate how idioms can preserve words which have otherwise gone out of use. Spick usually only occurs nowadays in the phrase spick and span – similarly kith in kith and kin.

Some idioms may have been drained of their original meaning but we go on using them despite having forgotten their origins. We say that someone is on tenterhooks even though we wouldn't recognize a tenterhook if we saw one, and we give somebody short shrift while probably unaware that it derives from giving someone a perfunctory confession and absolution before executing them. Nobody who combs their hair would describe the implement they use as a fine toothcomb, but we still use the phrase to describe an intensive search.

Despite the persistence of some idioms, plenty of them go out of use. Albert Hyamson's *Dictionary of English Phrases* (1922) lists many which are now obsolete. They include: *go to Bungay with you!* (= go away!), *to creep up someone's sleeve* (= to try to get into somebody's favour), *as wise as Doctor Dodipoll* (= stupid) and *the land of the two-legged mare* (= the gallows).

Idioms come from all kinds of pursuits, such as farming (buy a pig in a poke), the law (moot point), horse-riding (give rein to), warfare (stick to your guns), sport (a sticky wicket), card games (turn up trumps) and the human body (I'm all ears). Perhaps the largest number of idioms come from sailors and the sea, probably reflecting Britain's naval heritage: to be in the same boat, know the ropes, give someone a wide berth, shipshape and Bristol fashion, show a leg, three sheets to the wind, etc., etc.

Allusions

In the first edition of his famous *Dictionary of Phrase and Fable* (1870), Ebenezer Brewer noted that "We have all met with a number of familiar phrases, some of them 'as old as the hills', the meaning of which, though perfectly plain, it is difficult to connect with the words themselves".

Such phrases may be the kind of idioms we have just discussed, but they may be allusions: indirect or implicit references to what other people have said or written. The headings in almost any daily newspaper usually include several allusive phrases as well as idioms. Picking up a copy of the *Guardian* at random, I found plenty of allusions in headlines like: So foul a day, Mayhem as best laid plans go awry, The archdukes of hazard, Private Lives, Oldest ringer in town, Sins of the father, Any airport in a storm. These phrases allude respectively to quotations from Shakespeare and Robert Burns, the title of a TV series, a Noel Coward play, a 1981 hit song by Fred Wedlock, and two separate proverbs.

Allusions are widely used nowadays in popular writing, possibly because they can convey ideas quickly and vividly but often just as a way of letting your readers know that you are in tune with their interests. So you can imply your level of trendiness by alluding to popular songs, books, films and television programmes. Popular music is useful in this respect: a recent edition of a colour magazine included the headlines "Simply the Test" (from the title of a Tina Turner song) and "Mood Indigo" (alluding to a Duke Ellington tune as the heading for a fashion article). Kim Wilde's garden page is entitled "Wilde Side" – alluding either to Lou Reed's hit song "Walk on the Wild Side" or the film of the same name.

Darrell Holley's *Churchill's Literary Allusions* (1987) lists hundreds of examples to show how Winston Churchill's writings alluded to all kinds of authors: notably Victorian writers like Tennyson and Kipling as well as Macaulay (as a child, Churchill memorized the 1200 lines of Macaulay's *Lays of Ancient Rome*). The Bible featured heavily among allusions used by Churchill, including such biblical phrases as: *not one jot or tittle, clouds of witnesses, a millstone round one's neck,* and *no continuing city.* Churchill's Shakespearian allusions included: *that is the question, the course of true love never did run smooth,* and *age cannot wither her nor custom stale her infinite variety.*

In fact Shakespeare himself alluded to the Bible more than once. In *Hamlet* he wrote "There's a special providence in the fall of the sparrow" (recalling Matthew 10.29), and *Romeo and Juliet* includes "Do not swear at all" which echoes Matthew 5.34.

Some of these allusions are also quotations – which might be called direct allusions as distinct from the indirect ones (which may change the actual wording or don't necessarily say where the allusion comes from). When I was editing the *Oxford Dictionary of Modern Quotations*, I found that the 20th-century authors most frequently quoted were probably Bernard Shaw, Rudyard Kipling and A. E. Housman. The prolific and influential Shaw and Kipling are hardly surprising but Housman is more unexpected, since his output was comparatively small, but *A Shropshire Lad* clearly had a great effect on Housman's contemporaries.

Proverbs

Proverbs – like idioms – are an integral part of our language which we often take for granted. Someone once said that we don't need a definition of a proverb because we all know what it is, but it's actually quite hard to define a proverb. Cervantes said that proverbs are "short sentences drawn from long experience", while Lord John Russell is said to have described the proverb as "one man's wit and all men's wisdom".

The *Concise Oxford Dictionary* defines a proverb as "a short pithy saying in general use, stating a general truth or piece of advice". The *Oxford Dictionary of Proverbs* defines it slightly differently: as "a traditional saying which offers advice or presents a moral in a short and pithy manner". Proverb expert Archer Taylor noted that "Their range is limited to rather commonplace observations, but most of us are rather commonplace, too".

Many proverbs contain a metaphorical allusion, conjuring up a picture – as in "A burnt child dreads the fire" or "There's many a slip between cup and lip". Other proverbs are comparatively straightforward pieces of advice: "Honesty is the best policy"; "So many men, so many opinions". This last illustrates another common characteristic of proverbs, which are often symmetrical or balanced in some way: repeating the same word, contrasting two different situations, or using rhyme, alliteration or assonance – as in "He who laughs last, laughs longest", "Better to wear out than to rust out", "Look before you leap" and "Fast bind, fast find".

Proverbs are found in many different languages, often expressing similar ideas. So our "Don't cast pearls before swine" is apparently matched by a Chinese proverb advising against playing a harp in front of a cow. Where we say "Don't cross the bridge till you come to it", the Chinese say "Dismantle the bridge shortly after crossing it". But the Chinese seem to think differently from us when they say "Have a mouth as sharp as a dagger but a heart as soft as tofu", whereas we might advise "Speak softly and carry a big stick". In fact Chinese proverbs seem to have become legendary sources of wisdom, so that people will back up a statement (however implausible) by claiming that it's "in the words of an old Chinese proverb". The *Oxford Dictionary of Proverbs* says rather primly "There is no foundation to the ascription of Chinese origin" in a 1927 quotation which reads: "*Chinese proverb*, One picture is worth a thousand words".

Definitions of proverbs tend to state that they encapsulate truth or wisdom, but many proverbs seem to contradict one another. Should you believe "All things come to those who wait" or "Time and tide wait for no man", and "Strike while the iron is hot" or "He who hesitates is lost"? Why should "Absence make the heart grow fonder" if "Out of sight is out of mind"?

Quiz 4

Here is a list of proverbs. Try to think of proverbs that contradict what these say. For example, if the proverb is "Two's company, three's a crowd", you could come up with "The more the merrier".

1. Actions speak louder than words.
2. You can't teach an old dog new tricks.
3. Many hands make light work.
4. Clothes make the man.
5. Never look a gift horse in the mouth.
6. Opposites attract.
7. What will be, will be.
8. The road to hell is paved with good intentions.
9. Too many cooks spoil the broth.
10. The grass is always greener on the other side of the fence.

Rhetoric

Rhetoric has a bad reputation nowadays. It usually occurs in such phrases as "false rhetoric" or "misleading rhetoric", suggesting that it is an old-fashioned word for what is now known as "spin".

Yet for centuries, rhetoric was not only highly respected but formed an essential element of education. Its study arose in the 4th century BC, when Aristotle wrote his *On Rhetoric*. In this sense, *rhetoric* meant the art of using language convincingly or eloquently. Aristotle and other pioneers of rhetoric (like Cicero and Quintilian) believed that you could teach people how to speak or write persuasively, and the Sophists set up schools of rhetoric in fifth-century Athens.

From the Middle Ages onwards, education was based on the seven liberal arts, which were divided into the Quadrivium (arithmetic, geometry, astronomy and music) and the Trivium (rhetoric, grammar and logic). The concept of the liberal arts explains why we call some university graduates "Bachelor of Arts" or "Master of Arts".

"Rhetoric" was still a subject at some schools and universities until comparatively recently. I. A. Richards wrote in *The Philosophy of Rhetoric* (1936): "Rhetoric…is the dreariest and the least profitable part of the waste that the unfortunate travel through in Freshman English". And Rhetoric is apparently still the name of the top class at the Roman Catholic school Stonyhurst College.

Rhetoric didn't mean misleading oratory but simply effective communication: the handling of words to express yourself clearly or even eloquently. In this sense, it comes close to what we now more often call "style". And it embraces what we call "figures of speech": devices to make our communications more effective, persuasive or eloquent.

Figures of speech comprise anything that deviates from straightforward expression. So "The cat sat on the mat" is a simple statement, but it is more vivid if we add a simile: "The cat sat on the mat like a ball of black wool".

The simile and the metaphor are probably the figures of speech which most people know. As E. M. Forster said: "Only connect", and we often make connections between things when writing or speaking. We use similes which make comparisons ("He is like a bear with a sore head"; "You look as pretty as a picture") or we leave out such words as "like" and "as" to create metaphors ("He's a bear in the mornings"; "She's an English rose").

Metaphors are probably the commonest figures of speech in English. In fact many individual words got their present meaning through metaphors. The word *ponder* comes from a Latin root that meant "to weigh"; *explain* originally meant "to spread out"; *postpone* comes from two Latin words meaning "to place after"; and *attract* meant "to draw towards".

We often use metaphors without being aware of it – for example, when we resort to idioms like *pave the way, sift the evidence* and *one foot in the grave*. The biggest danger in metaphors is found in "mixed metaphors", which we consider in the next section.

There are a lot more figures of speech besides metaphors and similes. Henry Peacham's *Garden of Eloquence* (1577) enumerated nearly 200 figures, including bomphiologia, hypotiposis, prosographia, sermocinatio and topothesia.

However outlandish these words may appear, Peacham listed many figures of speech that we still use today. For example, there is metastasis, which Peacham says occurs "when we turn back those things that are objected against us, to them that laid them unto us" (e.g. "Talk about greedy! Who ate all the pies?")

Even if you didn't realise it, you have probably used synecdoche, where part of something is substituted for the whole (e.g. calling your car your "wheels"). You may even have used epizeuxis, the emphatic repetition of a word ("It was my brother – yes – my brother, who caused all the trouble"). And few people can boast that they have never resorted to hyperbole ("He's the greatest!").

Antonomasia is the name for that figure of speech in which we substitute an epithet or title for someone's name (e.g. calling Shakespeare "The Bard") or we use a proper name to evoke a particular characteristic ("A Daniel come to judgement!").

Anaphora or symploce is the term for another commonly-used rhetorical device: repeating one or more words or phrases for emphasis ("Where there is hatred, let me sow love; Where there is injury, pardon").

My favourite figure of speech mentioned by Henry Peacham is zeugma, which I somehow remember from my schooldays. The OED defines it as "A figure by which a single word is made to refer to two or more words in the sentence; esp. when properly applying in sense to only one of them, or applying to them in different senses". The example which is inexplicably imprinted on my mind is "She left in tears and a sedan chair".

Mixed metaphors

Having mentioned metaphors in the previous section, it seems necessary to look at one way in which they are often misused: as "mixed metaphors". These are groups of two or more metaphors which conjure up conflicting pictures. Perhaps the most notorious example occurred in a parliamentary speech by the Dublin politician Sir Boyle Roche (1743-1807) who said: "Mr Speaker, I smell a rat; I see him forming in the air and darkening the sky; but I'll nip him in the bud".

This is a mixed metaphor: a collection of incongruous imagery that sounds nonsensical. It confuses us if we are expected to summon up images that conflict with one another in our minds. In *The Complete Plain Words*, Sir Ernest Gowers quotes "The sacred cows have come home to roost with a vengeance" as a stock example of the mixed metaphor. He adds: "The statesman who said that sections of the population were being squeezed flat by inflation was not then in his happiest vein,...nor the enthusiastic scientist who announced the discovery of a virgin field pregnant with possibilities".

It is only too easy to mix metaphors, as Shakespeare did when he made Hamlet say "To take arms against a sea of troubles". Joseph Addison's *Letter from Italy* included: "I bridle in my struggling Muse with pain,/ That longs to launch into a bolder strain" – which Samuel Johnson criticized in his *Lives of the Poets*, saying: "To bridle a goddess is no very delicate idea...She is in the first line a horse, in the second a boat; and the care of the poet is to keep his horse or his boat from singing".

Politicians seem particularly susceptible to mixing their metaphors. Ernest Bevin is credited with "Your bread and butter will be cut from under your feet", while an earlier MP – O'Conor Power – said "Since the government has let the cat out of the bag, there is nothing to be done but to take the bull by the horns". In a debate on foreign policy, a certain Mr Cotton said "At one stage of the negotiations, a great European struggle was so imminent that it only required a spark to let slip the dogs of war". More recently, the MP for Bedford South-West said on the radio: "It all depends on whether there are any more hot potatoes waiting to come over the horizon". In 1987, the president of the National Farmers' Union said on television: "The butter mountain has been in the pipeline for some time".

Some Americans seem to have a slightly different concept of mixed metaphors. They describe as mixed metaphors what most of us would call malapropisms – simply transferring a word or phrase from one metaphor to another, ill-matched metaphor. This applies to confusions like "We'll burn that bridge when we come to it" (an uncomfortable collision of burning one's bridges and crossing them); "We're only scratching the iceberg"; "We'll tell everyone eventually but for now we'll keep it under tabs"; and "You don't have to be a rocket surgeon to work that out". The internet even advertises an American game of Mixed Metaphor Bingo, consisting of cards bearing such phrases as "Let's get down to brass roots", "He grabbed the bull by the tail" and "Rome wasn't burned in a day".

If you want to turn mixed metaphors into a game, you can simply try to construct a paragraph containing as many examples as possible. I'm sure you can do better than my quick attempt: "I ferreted out the truth that the sword of Damocles was hovering over my Pandora's box, and I was not out of the wood by a long chalk. My escutcheon was crawling with sins that could not be washed away by putting the clock back".

If you want more of a challenge, try writing verse full of mixed metaphors, like W. R. Espy's poem crammed with bodily images:

> If I should seek your hand – I lack the cheek;
> Ah, let your bowels of compassion start!
> Lend me a leg up! Quickly! – lest I seek
> A toehold in some softer, warmer heart.

Oxymorons

Mixed metaphors are just one example of contradictory statements, but there are many others – not always accidental. One deliberate form of contradiction is the oxymoron: a phrase that seems to convey two conflicting ideas at once.

Most people have heard of Noel Coward's musical show *Bitter Sweet* and his song *Poor Little Rich Girl*. Both of these are oxymorons. How can something be bitter as well as sweet? How can a rich girl also be poor?

The word *oxymoron* is itself an oxymoron. It comes from two Latin words meaning "sharp" and "dull".

Although many oxymorons sound paradoxical, they can express truths about the mixed emotions we often feel, and they are often used in literature. Milton's *Paradise Lost* spoke about "darkness visible". Tennyson wrote "Faith unfaithful kept him falsely true". In *Romeo and Juliet*, Shakespeare's heroine said that parting is "such sweet sorrow", while Romeo talked of "heavy lightness, serious vanity". And Hamlet was the first person to say "I must be cruel to be kind".

Everyday speech is full of such contradictions. We say that something is done "accidentally on purpose". We go shopping for paper tablecloths, plastic glasses, jumbo shrimps, white chocolate or fresh frozen peas. We might even find a "live recording" of Simon & Garfunkel's *Sound of Silence*.

Sometimes the incongruity is hidden in the origins of words. We might speak about a typed manuscript, forgetting that manuscript properly means something written by hand. Perhaps we like the sound of the pianoforte, which comes from a pair of Italian words meaning "soft" and "loud".

Often the contradiction is in the eye of the beholder, who sees a paradox where others see nothing unusual. You may think there is something oxymoronic about phrases like painless childbirth, safe sex, background music, the United Nations, military intelligence or benevolent dictator.

My favourite oxymoron was coined by the comedian Benny Hill, who described someone as "a shy and retiring used-car salesman".

Quiz 5

Which of these words can be paired together to make 14 oxymorons?
Baby, cable, difference, dry, fiction, grand, health, heavyweight, ice,
idiot, ill, inside, light, link, missing, nothings, order, out, pretty, random,
same, savant, science, student, sweet, teacher, ugly, wireless.

8

Puns

Daft definitions

In the previous chapter under "Clichés", I mentioned Gustave Flaubert's *Dictionnaire des Idées Reçues*, which consisted of definitions of hackneyed expressions and thoughts (e.g. "*Weather,* eternal topic of conversation").

The American satirist Ambrose Bierce compiled *The Devil's Dictionary* which contains many such ironical definitions. He defines patriotism as "Combustible rubbish ready for the torch of anyone ambitious to illumine his name," and patience as "a minor form of despair, disguised as a virtue".

Irony is an invaluable ingredient in concocting new definitions, as in Bernard Rosenberg's *Dictionary for the Disenchanted* (1972), which defines credibility gap as "The growing suspicion that once in a while the Administration may not be lying" and foreign aid as "Taxing poor people in rich countries for the benefit of rich people in poor countries". Beachcomber (alias J. B. Morton) suggested these new definitions: "*Arctic conditions*, a cold day in England" and "*No exit*, a sign indicating the most convenient way out of a building".

The literary competitions in such magazines as the *New Statesman* and the *Spectator* often challenge readers to devise new definitions for existing words. One such competition asked readers to supply definitions of sports, which produced:

> *Golf,* a pitch 'n' sink drama.
> *Boxing*, the sport of dukes.
> *Whippet racing*, the curs of the working classes.
> *Weight-lifting*, careless rupture.

These redefinitions of existing words and phrases are known as Daft Definitions or Daffy Definitions (or Daffynitions), and they frequently depend upon puns. Here are some of my favourites:

Travelogue, a dug-out canoe.

Myth, a female moth.

Hamlet, a baby pig.

Bacteria, the rear entrance to a cafeteria.

Boomerang, what you say to frighten a meringue.

The BBC Radio 4 series *I'm Sorry I Haven't a Clue* has come up with such definitions as these:

Gripe, what Australians make wine from.

MacAdam, the first Scotsman.

Stucco, hitherto unknown Marx Brother.

Carpentry, a way in for ornamental fish.

When I noticed that the *Nursing Times* was printing punning definitions of medical terms (e.g. *Dilate*, to live long), I sent them these suggestions:

Anaesthetic, Oscar Wilde.

Gallstone, it annoys Tony.

Vaseline, an inscription on a Greek vase.

Testicle, an exploratory tickle.

The most impressive definitions are those that cleverly sum up a word, such as "*Journalist,* a pitiable wretch who writes with his editor's tongue in his cheek" and "*Pessimist,* one who, being told that we live in the best of all possible worlds, fears that is true". A more punchy definition of *pessimist* is "someone who fears the best," reminding us that the best new definitions are often the most concise. Ambrose Bierce hit the target with "*Twice*, once too often". Such aphoristic definitions are often salted by witty punning, as in "*Cold storage,* a handkerchief" and "*Incense*, holy smoke".

Why not create your own new definitions? One possibility is to try defining the names of trades or professions, giving results like:

Statistician, someone who counts for a lot.

Milkman, one who crates a disturbance.

Dentist, someone who is often down in the mouth.

Feminist, a woman who never fails to hit the male on the head.

Childminder, someone who doesn't mind children.

The most wonderful new definitions are probably those that are downright perverse or totally daffy, like "*Bricklayer,* confused chicken" and "*Height,* depth upside down". When I was a youngster, I loved the ramblings of a contributor to the *Saturday Evening Post* who called himself Colonel Stoopnagle. His weird explanations included "A clock is something they have in an office, so you can tell how late you wish you weren't in the morning, what time to go out to lunch before and come back after, and how long before you can start stopping work by stalling along until".

Perhaps Colonel Stoopnagle's masterpiece was his dissertation on a circle: "No wonder they call it a circle – it's so round! Notice how the inside comes precisely to the line and not one whit farther. And how the outside can't possibly get in. No corners is one of the principal things about a circle. An oval has no corners, too, but they're not nearly as no corners as a circle has. Circles are nice because we can go around in them. Hardly anybody ever goes around in squares. Every single place on the outside of a circle is the same distance from the centre as every other place. You can't say that about a parallelopiped".

Quiz 6

Try to think of punning definitions for the following words and phrases. There are no "right" answers, but some possibilities are suggested in the "Answers" section.
1. Accidental. 2. Auctioneer. 3. Champagne. 4. Farcical. 5. Fast food. 6. Innuendo. 7. Life jacket. 8. Maritime. 9. Neurosis. 10. Relief. 11. Servile. 12. Stalemate.

Punning names

One of the most childish but irresistible pastimes is the one where you devise suitable punning names for the authors of imaginary books. For some reason, the best-known example is *The Broken Window* by Eva Brick. *Foulsham's Fun Book* (1933) had a list of "Books You Simply Must Read", including *Cutting It Fine* by Moses Lawn, *The Corn* by Honor Foote, *The Cliff Tragedy* by Eileen Dover, *Knighted* by Watts E. Dunn, *Wine and Women* by Rex Holmes, and *The Song of the Shirt* by Dryden Aird.

Other memorable books include *The Dentist* by Phil Macavity, *French Windows* by Pattie O'Dors, *Never Borrow* by Nora Lenderby, *Fitted Carpets* by Walter Wall, and *The Lion Tamer* by Claude Bottom. Authors can also have initials instead of first names, as in *Astronomy* by I. C. Stars, *All About Dogs* by K. Nine, *Leftovers* by E. Tittup and *Loud Rumblings* by M. T. Tumm.

A similar game challenges players to think of suitable names for people with particular occupations or interests. So appropriate names for musicians might include Grace Note, Clarrie Nett, Amanda Lynne, Carol Singer, Nelson Dorma, Coral Evensong, Ann Dante, Ron Dough, Sarah Nade, Wyn de Band, Chris Shendo, G. String and P. Anno (not forgetting Our Monica). Suitable names for weather forecasters would be Gale Force, Hugh Middity, P. Super, Ty Phoon, Cy Clone, Sonny Spells, Harry Cane and Ellie Mentz. I like to think that somewhere there is a mathematician named Lois Carmen Denominator.

Returning to the subject of book titles, there is fun to be had from imagining books that were failures because they had titles that never appealed to readers. These might include Charles Dickens's *A Tale of One City*, J. R. R. Tolkien's *The Lord of the Things*, Thackeray's *Vanity Case*, John Steinbeck's *The Wrath of Grapes*, Adolf Hitler's *My Camp*, Oscar Wilde's *The Importance of Being Serious*, and Tony Augarde's *Oxford Guide to Worm Games*. We can also try to make books more interesting by "sexing them up" – rendering their titles more suggestive, as in Thomas Hardy's *Jude the Obscene*, Shakespeare's *Romeo and Julian*, and Evelyn Waugh's *Maidenhead Revisited*.

Some genuine books have been published with titles that sound more suggestive than intended. For instance, James Laver's *Memorable Balls* (1954) was a study of fashionable pastimes, and Mea Allen's *The Hookers of Kew* (1967) was a biography of a family of botanists. Rose Fyleman's *Gay Go Up* (1929) was innocent enough when it was published but it might be misconstrued today – as would *How It Was Done at Stow School* (1862), *The Ups and Downs of Lady Di* (1907) and even Macaulay's *Lays of Ancient Rome* (1842). Perhaps the best-known example of an unfortunate title is Baden-Powell's *Scouting for Boys* (1908).

Since 1978, *The Bookseller* has run an annual competition to find the most incredible title of a book published in that year. Winners have included *The Joy of Chickens*, *The Theory of Lengthwise Rolling*, and *Braces Owner's Manual*. Earlier titles that might have qualified include *Truncheons: Their Romance and Reality*, *The Wife-Beater's Manual*, and *The Diagnosis of the Acute Abdomen in Rhyme*. I remember owning a book entitled *The Culture of the Abdomen*.

Quiz 7

Here are ten imaginary book titles for which you are invited to supply a suitable surname for the author.
1. *Wait a Moment by Arthur...*
2. *Shipwreck by Mandy...*
3. *The Merry Widow by Gail...*
4. *Wickedness by Evelyn...*
5. *Horse riding by Jim...*
6. *Travelling by Wanda... & Sally...*
7. *My mother-in-law by George...*
8. *Rossini Operas by Barbara...*
9. *Mountains of South America by Ann...*
10. *A Stagnant Pool in Australia by Bill...*

Punning headlines

Tabloid newspapers seem to have an obsession with using puns in their headlines. The worst offender is the *Sun*, which tries to insert puns – often very weak and unimaginative puns – into virtually every headline. Examples I have noted include WATCH THIS SPICE (about the Spice Girls) and WHO IS ABBEY'S BREAST FRIEND? (about busty actress Abbey Clancy). An item about Keira Knightley's new spectacles described them as giving her "specs appeal" and the headline was: KNIGHTLEY'S A GLASS ACT. Some of the *Sun*'s puns are ridiculously forced, like the one about Amy Winehouse showing her brassière: AMY BRA-VES THE COLD.

The *Daily Mirror* can be almost as atrocious, with such punning headlines as IT'S WHETSUN, PLATE EXPECTATIONS, THAT'S ENOUGH GOUDA CAUSES (an article mentioning cheese), and EWE'LL BE IN TROUBLE (about a stolen sheep). The only headline that showed much ingenuity topped a story about an ambitious euphonium player: THE OOMPAH STRIKES BACK.

Headlines can be very clever, like the classic words that headed a football report about the Caledonian Thistle team unexpectedly beating Celtic: SUPER CALLY GO BALLISTIC, CELTIC ARE ATROCIOUS. Another nice line headed a story about a shortage of books in the Essex town of Ongar: BOOKS LACK IN ONGAR.

In the days when I used to write reviews of pop records for the *Oxford Times*, I was proud of suggesting the headline: NOW IS THE WINTER OF OUR DISCO CONTENT.

In fact quality newspapers are almost as likely as tabloids to use weak puns in headlines. One issue of the *Observer*'s "Review" section committed these horrors: THERE'S ONE FAUN EVERY MINUTE, THE BOOK OF COMMON PRAIRIE and IT'LL BE ALL RIOT ON THE NIGHT. I preferred the *Evening Standard*'s heading for a damning review of a French musical of *Notre Dame de Paris*: "It's a crock, monsieur" (punning on *croque-monsieur*, the French version of Welsh rabbit).

Punning headlines are nothing new. Back in 1995, Fritz Spiegl was complaining about their frequency, noting that "Puns can be clever but simply misspelling words or replacing them with homonyms – write/right/rite, rain/reign/rein – is neither clever nor funny." Spiegl tells of a friend who attended a course on "How to write accurate, punchy headlines". Spiegl says: "Was he warned against clichés? No, just the opposite. When sub-editing a recipe for, say, oat cakes, the appropriate headline they taught him was 'Oat cuisine'. For chocolate? 'Choc tactics'. For eggs? 'Eggstra special' or 'Eggstravaganza'."

Fritz Spiegl admits that some headlines are ingenious. During the cash-for-questions scandal, the *Guardian* had SELL ME THE SAME OLD TORY. And an article about balaclavas becoming fashionable for winter was headed PULL THE WOOL OVER YOUR EYES.

There are several games you can play with headlines. One is to devise headlines which summarize the plot of a famous book, play or film. Thus PRINCE DIES AFTER KILLING HIS UNCLE might describe the end of Shakespeare's *Hamlet*.

Quiz 8

Which famous writings might be summarized by the following headlines?
1. INDIAN DENIES CAVE ASSAULT CHARGE. 2. AIR ACCIDENT MAROONS CHILDREN ON DESERT ISLAND. 3. STRIPPER WINS ONCE-IN-A-LIFETIME PRIZE. 4. QUEEN ADMITS: I FANCIED BOTTOM. 5. ALIENS INVADE WOKING.

Advertising puns

Commercial names can be intriguing – or puzzling. In my locality, there is a firm called Aasvogel Recycling. Did it choose its name because of some connection with vultures, since *aasvogel* is a South African word for a vulture? Or was it simply so that it would appear first in any alphabetical list – for example, in the Yellow Pages? I have also seen the name "Justin White" on vans in Oxford and wondered whether the business was started by a man with this name or if it is simply a clever punning title for a cleaning firm.

Back in 1912, Walter Jerrold in his *Book of Famous Wits* noted that "the pun...seems to flourish in the field of advertisement", adding: "I imagine the typical anti-punster as walking about with a 'Waukenphast' boot on one foot, a 'Phiteesi' on the other, smoking a 'Uneeda' cigar, and peering about through 'Eusebius' spectacles for anything like a pun at which he can sneer".

Puns have certainly been plentiful in advertisemernts of the past. Nigel Rees's *Book of Slogans and Catchphrases* cites "Do you know Uneeda biscuit?" from 1898, and an advertisement for Morton salt from 1911 which promised "When it rains, it pours".

We all know "My Goodness, My Guinness!" from the firm which has also used such slogans as "Tall, dark and have some" and "Cool, calm and collect it". For many years, Bovril was advertised with posters showing a shipwrecked passenger clinging to a Bovril jar, with the caption "Bovril prevents that sinking feeling". And the famous slogan for the British Egg Marketing Board – "Go to work on an egg" – has been ascribed to novelist Fay Weldon.

Present-day advertisements seem to use fewer puns. Perhaps their ambiguous nature is thought unsuitable for an industry that tries to present itself as honest, avoiding double-talk. Claude C. Hopkins wrote in *My Life in Advertising*: "Frivolity has no place in advertising. Nor has humour… People do not buy from clowns". Many television commercials employ humour but puns are not particularly common nowadays.

However, my mention of the Yellow Pages reminds us that puns are still prevalent in the naming of commercial firms. You can spend many idle hours leafing through your local edition of Yellow Pages on the lookout for such puns – and they are especially prevalent in the names of hairdressers. The Oxford directory includes A Cut Above, Ahead of Hair, Aristocuts, The Crop Shop, Curl Up and Dye, Headfirst, Headstart, Short Cuts, Upper Cut and (my favourite) Hair 2 Dye 4. Men's barbers are named Baldys, Men's Room and Over the Top.

Collectors of puns have frequently commented upon this tendency for hairdressers to adopt punny names. America seems to be full of them: The Clip Joint, Cliptomania, The Curl Friend, Fresh Hair, From Hair to Eternity, Hair After, Hair Apparent, Hair Force, Hairodynamics, Hair's What's Happening, Hairways, Mane Event, Mein Hair, On the Hair, The Razor's Edge, Scissors Palace, Shy Locks. Londonderry in New Hampshire has a shop called Londonderry Hair, while Lansing in Michigan has the dubious Public Hair Ltd. Some hairdressers have rather unappealing names, like Blood, Sweat & Shears, Le Guillotine Hairstylists and Samson & Delilah.

Local British beauty salons also have some inventive names: The Beauty Spot, Face Facts and Skin Deep, although I worry about the rightness of a beauty shop called Clydesdales, which conjures up images of heavy horses. Introduction agencies in our Yellow Pages include 2meetyou.com.Ltd. and Dining to Meet You. Buckingham boasts a restaurant called the Eggstraordinary Eating House.

Double entendres

Beauty is in the eye of the beholder. So is decency – and rudery. If anyone finds something indecent in the examples of wordplay here, they have only themselves to blame, since the pure-minded will fail to see anything rude.

We are talking about *double entendres*, which – as the phrase suggests – implies sayings that have more than one meaning. This might make us think of puns, which use language's ambiguity to play with words that have similar meanings or sounds. However, the *double entendre* usually has an extra dimension: that one of two or more possible interpretations is obscene or risqué. The advantage of this form of pun is that, if someone seems offended by it, you can innocently pretend that you never meant it to be interpreted in a rude sense.

In their 1978 book *Upon the Pun*, Hammond & Hughes rather laboriously define the *double entendre*: "The *double entendre* is a play on words, one meaning of which is lewd: 'Did you hear about the sleepy bride who couldn't stay awake for a second?' This sentence contains a play on the word *second*. One meaning is 'Did you hear about the sleepy bride who couldn't stay awake for a second (moment of time)?' The other is 'Did you hear about the sleepy bride who couldn't stay awake for a second (bout of lovemaking)?' "

Double entendres are now so commonplace that we almost take them for granted. The "Carry On" series of films constructed their comedy largely out of the *double entendre*: knowing that the audience will probably laugh at anything that can be interpreted as referring to a bodily part or function. For example, when Kenneth Williams asserted in a "Carry On" film that "Old birds need a lot of stuffing", we know that he is not necessarily referring to turkeys.

Double entendres have been used for centuries. Many lines by Shakespeare are capable of being taken in this way. In *Hamlet*, when the audience is assembling to watch *The Mousetrap*, Hamlet says to Ophelia: "Lady, shall I lie in your lap?" Ophelia replies "No, my lord", and Hamlet ripostes "I mean, my head upon your lap". Hamlet goes on to make even more ambiguous statements, emphasising the sexual undercurrent in the scene. Other notable Shakespearian examples occur in *Twelfth Night* (when Malvolio is reading a letter supposedly from Olivia) and in Mercutio's verbal sparring with Juliet's nurse in *Romeo and Juliet*.

Prudery – at least, superficial prudery – clamped down in the 17th century, which was obsessed with "correctness". S. Ullmann's *Principles of Semantics* describes how the 17th-century *précieuses* were so desperate to avoid any hint of rudeness that "a group of six American musicians had to be called a 'quartet' since a 'sextet' would have been too suggestive".

One thinks of the Victorians as prim and proper but apparently W. S. Gilbert (of Gilbert & Sullivan) wrote a drama including a servant called Scrotum, described as "a wrinkled retainer". The music-hall singer Marie

Lloyd was allegedly told by a theatre manager that she should not sing a song which included the line: "She sits among the cabbages and peas". Marie responded by changing the line to: "She sits among the lettuces and leeks". Similarly robust humour appeared in the captions of seaside postcards drawn by such artists as Donald McGill (e.g. "I can't see my little Willie").

Some of the best *double entendres* are unintentional, like the newspaper headline "Population of USA broken down by age and sex". The most notorious inadvertent example is Robert Browning's reference in *Pippa Passes* to "Cowls and twats, Monks and nuns, in a cloister's moods" – in the mistaken belief that *twat* meant a garment worn by a nun.

Charles Dickens's *Martin Chuzzlewit* describes how Tom Pinch, the church organist, loved Mary Graham: "She touched his organ, and from that bright epoch even it, the old companion of his happiest hours, incapable as he had thought of elevation, began a new and deified existence".

9

Slang

Slinging words around

If puns have fun with the sounds and meanings of words, we might enquire what slang is, as it seems to imply the same sort of irreverence towards words.

The trouble is that it is almost impossible to define slang, because it means different things to different people. Etymologically, slang seems most likely to be language that is *slung* about. The American poet Carl Sandburg famously said "Slang is a language that rolls up its sleeves, spits on its hands, and goes to work".

Jonathan Green calls it "the language of the rebel, the outlaw, the despised, the marginal, the young". This suggests that it is a separate vocabulary employed by a particular group of people, yet slang can also be language that is widely used by many different people but is distinguished by being very informal – as *Fowler's Modern English Usage* says "at the extreme end of informality". Slang might be defined as language that is unsuitable in formal situations. It may not be a good idea to use slang expressions when applying for a job or addressing the Queen.

So slang is disrespectful: a reaction against politeness and propriety. This is certainly true of the rude words that make up a significant proportion of slang. These are sometimes called four-letter words (we all know the "C word" and the "F word", even though some people would deny ever using them). In fact such words are so well known that they increasingly appear in speech and even in print. It seems pointless to try disguising them as "f***" or "f***ing", when they are so familiar in everyday parlance. Words like *crap*, which were once considered obscene slang, have entered standard English as a result of being used to mean nonsense or rubbish.

Slang – like the rest of the language – changes with time. In fact many slang words come in and out of the language remarkably quickly. As a term of approval, *groovy* was soon replaced by *fab*, which in its turn gave way to *ace, awesome, brill, cool*, etc.

Slang is now used so widely in books, newspapers, films and on TV that it is no longer the private or restricted language that it used to be. Many slang words percolate into standard English – like *flapper* (which, in its turn, is now only used historically), *crestfallen, stodgy* and the more recent *gay* (for homosexual). Dr Johnson characterised *bogus, clever, joke* and *snob* as "low words" but they have now been assimilated into standard English. J. C. Hotten's *Dictionary of Modern Slang, Cant and Vulgar Words* (1859) includes *dumb-found, randy, scrumptious, starchy* ("stuck-up, high-notioned, showily dressed, disdainful, cross") and *rather!* ("a ridiculous street exclamation synonymous with yes"). *Bus* and *pub* started life as slang shortenings of *omnibus* and *public house* but they are now found more often than the longer forms. Other words (like *arse* and *tit*) start as standard English but later come to be regarded as slang.

Many dictionaries continue to regard words like *booze, lousy* and *raunchy* as "slang", despite their use by a majority of the population. For example, *The Oxford Dictionary of Modern Slang* (1992) includes *rag trade*, even though most of us know what it means from the title of a TV sitcom in the early 1960s. *Dipstick* meaning a fool is in the same dictionary but, again, this is surely known and used widely from such TV series as *Only Fools and Horses*.

Anthony Burgess said that "The word slang...suggests the slinging of odd stones or dollops of mud at the windows of the stately home of linguistic decorum". Now that this stately home has been opened to the public, where does that leave slang?

There used to be a fairly clear gap between slang and standard English but, because that gap was primarily a class divide, the gap has become much narrower in our modern classless society. Most of us treat one another without the stiff formality of earlier times. If slang has become acceptable – even respectable – does the label have valid meaning any more?

Jargon

Now that we have shaken off the starchy attitudes of the past and so many slang expressions quickly become assimilated into standard English, perhaps there is no role for the label "slang" to describe language that is unsuited to formal contexts.

However, the term is still relevant in one of its earliest senses: as a word for the particular language of a group or profession. Many groups of people have a vocabulary particular to their trade or pastime. So you can talk about underworld slang and university slang, or the slang of doctors, the police, market traders, computer users, schoolchildren, etc. An alternative term for this kind of specialized language is "jargon", although this can embrace the technical terms used in a particular job.

For example, as a part-time jazz musician, I am familiar with such recondite slang as *axe* for a musical instrument, *horn* for any musical instrument that you blow, *dots* for sheet music, *sideman* for a member of a band, and even *liquorice stick* for a clarinet. But other jazz slang has entered the mainstream language – like *gig* for a musical engagement or performance, *bebop* for a style of jazz, or *Satchmo* as a nickname for Louis Armstrong (a shortened form of *satchel-mouth*).

Most professions and specialized areas of interest have their own unique language, which outsiders may regard as slang. Yet this kind of slang often crosses over into standard English. At one time it was only computer nerds who used terms like *hacking* and *surfing* for particular computer activities but now even Luddites like myself are familiar with these expressions. Reports of the Falklands War familiarized us with the military slang word *yomping*, while film and television dramas have made us aware of drug-users' slang like *fix, grass, junkie, reefer, shoot up* and *smack*.

This kind of slang arises naturally because of the special things that these groups talk about. But it can also be created as a deliberate way of excluding outsiders, who are not intended to understand a restricted jargon. "Cant" and "argot" are names for the languages that criminals developed as a way of talking secretly with one another. Cant expressions that have percolated into standard English include *bilk* (to swindle), *hit* (to kill), *monicker* or *moniker* (a name) and *old lag*.

Another brand of argot is Polari (or Parlyaree), a "secret" slang used particularly among entertainers, sailors and the gay community. It became less of a secret when it was used in the conversations of Julian and Sandy in the sixties' BBC radio series *Round the Horne*. Its vocabulary includes *bona* (nice), *eek* (face), *lallies* (legs), *omee* (man), *palone* (woman), *troll* (wander) and *vada* (look). So, in a scene in a lawcourt, Julian or Sandy might say "Omees and palones of the jury, vada well at the eek of the poor omee who stands before you, his lallies trembling".

The word "slang" may be appropriate to describe swear words or obscenities which are still regarded as beyond the pale, although their number is decreasing rapidly. Bernard Shaw shocked the nation in 1914 when he made Eliza Doolittle say "Not bloody likely" in *Pygmalion*. He justified its use by saying that "the word 'bloody'...is in common use as an expletive by four-fifths of the English nation, including many highly-educated persons". By 1956, when *Pygmalion* was transformed into *My Fair Lady*, the word had lost its power to shock.

High society can no longer pretend to be appalled by words like *bloody* when even Prince Charles uses the word – and Princess Anne tells journalists to "naff off" (as she famously did in 1982). When Harold Pinter's *The Caretaker* was first performed in 1960, I remember feeling slight surprise (but also amusement) at a monk telling a tramp to "piss off". But that was many years ago. Events like the Lady Chatterley trial and televised utterances by the Sex Pistols and Kenneth Tynan helped to create a more permissive society. Nobody seemed outraged when a more recent TV programme was entitled *Antisocial Old Buggers*.

Some words used to describe sexual matters can still be labelled as slang, although most people accept them as normal and inoffensive.

C. S. Lewis put his finger on the problem of sexual vocabulary when he said that "You are forced to choose between the language of the nursery, the gutter and the anatomy class". The nursery words seem too babyish and the anatomical vocabulary sounds stilted, so we often resort to the gutter words. Witnesses in the Lady Chatterley trial suggested that the F word describes an entirely natural process.

Labels like "slang" or "informal" or "colloquial" may be useful in dictionaries as a sort of warning – just as people may like to be warned if they are being ungrammatical or using words incorrectly. Foreign learners of English, for example, need to know how they should address their teacher. Without such guidance, they may use unsuitable words like guv, boss or mate. But the democratisation of language means that most words are potentially used by all kinds of people, and "slang" has become too blunt an instrument to be useful except in an increasingly limited range of situations.

Rhyming slang

When the preceding article on slang was printed in *The Oxford Times*, it was given a title which reminded me of one type of slang that deserves attention. The heading was "Linguistic decorum? I should coco..." The phrase "I should coco (or cocoa)" is rhyming slang for "I should say so". It also occurs in longer forms: "I should coffee and cocoa" and "I should tea and cocoa". This phenomenon is typical of rhyming slang, where expressions often start out as phrases but are then shortened to a single word. Perhaps the best–known example of rhyming slang is *apples and pears* (meaning stairs), which is commonly shortened to *apples*.

Rhyming slang probably originated in the 19th century in east London, where such people as street traders and dockers (and perhaps criminals) started substituting rhyming words for other words – either to conceal from outsiders what they were saying to their friends or simply because they enjoyed playing about with words (Cockneys have always been credited with having the gift of the gab). Hotten's *Dictionary of Modern Slang* (1859) says "The rhyming slang was introduced about 12 or 15 years ago".

Most frequently in rhyming slang, a single word is replaced by one or more words that rhyme with it. The substitution may be a single word (*Joanna* = piano), a combination of two words (*daisy roots* = boots), a phrase of three or more words (*trouble and strife* = wife; *open the door* = 44; *on your Tod Sloan* = alone) or the name of a person (*Ruby Murray* = curry; *Uncle Dick* = sick). These substitutions can be a bit of a mouthful, which explains why they are often abbreviated, so that *uncle* on its own comes to mean sick, while *on your tod* means alone.

Some words have more than one variant in rhyming slang – for instance, a judge can be a *Barnaby Rudge, chocolate fudge, inky smudge* or *smear and smudge*. And some slang words have more than one meaning, so that *porky* (short for *porky pie*) can mean a lie or an eye, while *raspberry* (in full *raspberry tart*) can indicate the heart or a rather rude word for the result of flatulence. Talking of rudery, it is interesting that words like *berk* (a fool) and *cobblers* (nonsense) have virtually become respectable, even though they originated as naughtily suggestive phrases (*Berkeley* or *Berkshire hunt* and *cobblers' awls*).

This sort of slang is sometimes called Cockney rhyming slang but Cockneys are not the only people who use it. In the 1950s, Iona and Peter Opie noted that "as far away as Newcastle, respectable children can be heard saying they are 'going for a ball of chalk' when setting out for a walk, and accusing someone of being a 'tea-leaf' when they mean a thief".

Scottish lexicographer Iseabail Macleod has observed that Scottish people have devised their own forms of rhyming slang, which wouldn't be readily understood in England: "For example, we say corned beef to mean 'deif', but beef doesn't rhyme with deaf. And 'pottit heid' means 'deid', which doesn't rhyme with the word dead". Rhyming slang is also found in the USA and Australia. In Britain, *butcher's* (short for butcher's hook) means a look, but in Australia it means crook, *i.e.* unwell.

Rhyming slang has an old-fashioned air about it but it has been kept in use by such things as films and television dramas portraying Cockney life. The seventies' TV series *The Sweeney* had a title that means "flying squad". One issue of the magazine *We Love Telly!* had a caption to an *EastEnders* photo reading "Zoe hits Chrissie in the boat race" (i.e. face). And a recent TV documentary showed a London driver saying "It's all gone Pete Tong" (i.e. wrong). New expressions are still being coined, so that you may encounter such modern allusions as *Millennium Dome* (=a comb), *Britney Spears* (=beers) and *Tony Blairs* (=flares, i.e. flared trousers). And rhyming slang is commonly heard in bingo halls, where *garden gate* means eight and *clickety-click* is 66.

As a challenge, I'll conclude with a short story for you to translate into standard English (the answer is below):

As I pulled on my daisy roots, my barnet fell over my boat-race, covering my mince pies and my bottle of beers. So I didn't hear the dog and bone when my trouble and strife called to tell me that the king's proctor said that she had Chalfont St Giles. Would you Adam and Eve it?

Translation
As I pulled on my boots, my hair fell over my face, covering my eyes and my ears. So I didn't hear the phone when my wife called to tell me that the doctor said that she had piles. Would you believe it?

Pig Latin and backslang

One of my favourite singers is Anita Belle Colton, better known to jazz fans as Anita O'Day. She adopted the latter name during the Great Depression, when she competed in dance marathons. She chose the name O'Day because it was "pig Latin" for "dough" – that is, the money she wanted to make.

Pig Latin originally meant incorrect Latin, and it was also called dog Latin or hog Latin. In the 19th century, it came to describe a kind of slang in which the first consonant (or consonants) of words are transferred to the end of those words and an extra syllable (usually *-ay*) is added. Thus *dough* was turned into *O'Day*, *give* becomes *ivgay* and *scratch* becomes *atchscray*. If a word begins with a vowel, you simply add -ay (or sometimes -way or -yay) on the end, strangely turning *essay* into *essay-ay* and *alley* into *alley-way*.

Most pig Latin sounds like gibberish, but some words have interesting results when thus transformed. For example, the word *be* becomes *eBay* (the name of a well-known internet trading site). *Ayspray* can be pig Latin for *prays* or *spray*.

Here are some more weird transformations created by pig Latin:

Trash...ashtray

Lover...overlay

Trice...ice tray

Wonder...under way

Devil...evil day

The *Oxford English Dictionary* includes the mainly American word *ixnay*, which is a pig Latin variant of *nix*, meaning to reject or deny (or as an adverb or interjection, meaning worthless or not at all). In the film *The Lion King*, Zazu says "Ixnay on the upidstay", which means "Stop being stupid". The *OED* currently omits *amscray*, which is a common American variation on *scram* (= go away), but it is apparently being included in the revised edition.

Someone has already translated the Bible into pig Latin! The first verse of *Genesis* (or rather Enesis-gay) is: "In-ay e-thay eginning-bay Od-gay eatedcray e-thay eaven-hay and-ay e-thay earth-ay".

The French have a similar kind of slang called loucherbem. It originated among Parisian butchers and got its name from *boucher*, the French for butcher. Like pig Latin, it transferred the first letter of a word to the end, put a new letter – usually L – at the beginning, and added a new suffix (like *-em* or *-uche*). So *boucher* became *loucherbem*, and *patron* turned into *latronpuche*. This language is also called *largonji*, which results from the similar transformation of the word *jargon*.

Loucherbem is found as early as 1837 in the *Memoirs* of Vidocq, a criminal-turned-police-collaborator, who recorded *Lorcefé* for the Parisian prison La Force, where he spent some time.

Some of these private languages were originally devised so that a group of people (such as tradesmen or schoolchildren) could converse without eavesdroppers understanding them. Such mysterious languages have been in use since the 16th century, when they were called "pedlar's French". One well-known example is backslang, a variety of slang in which words are pronounced backwards.

Backslang was first used by London costermongers in the 19th century, and later caught on amongst butchers and others. A butcher might say to his colleague: "Evig reh emos delo garcs dene", meaning "Give her some old scrag end".

Backslang gave us the common word *yob,* which was originally slang for *boy* but has come to mean a lout. If you wonder why the police are sometimes called *slops*, it is an adaptation of backslang *ecilop*.

Backslang turned the numbers under eight into *eno, oat, earth* (or *eerith), roaf* (or *ralph), evif, exis* and *nevis*. This shows how words could be adapted by adding or removing letters or changing the pronunciation if they created problems when reversed. So *shop* became *posh, butcher* became *richtub, balls* became *slabs,* and *head* became *deeache* or *dee-aitch*.

Iona & Peter Opie, in their *Lore and Language of Children* (1959), give the example "Uoy nac ess reh sreckin ginwosh" for "You can see her knickers showing".

The Opies describe several other ways in which secret languages are used to mystify or exclude outsiders. In Scarborough, they found teenage girls inserting "ag" before each vowel, to make their own secret patter, or "thageir agown pagattager". Children elsewhere used "eg" or "arag" in the same way.

Such secret languages have often been used by parents trying to prevent children knowing what they were talking about. In 1808, Elizabeth Grant wrote in her autobiography how parents had used a "how-vus do-vus language" until they realized the children had cracked the code, when the grown-ups adopted a new device of tacking "thegee" onto the end of every word.

At least one such originally "secret" expression has found its way into the *OED*: *F.H.B.* (= family hold back), which the OED dates from as early as 1911 and defines as "a colloquial intimation to the members of a family that their guests have first claim on the course or helping about to be served".

Blason populaire

Are you familiar with the phrase *blason populaire*? I encountered it in a publication by John Widdowson & Joanne Green, who wrote the enticingly-titled *Traditional Language Genres: Continuity and Change, 1950-2000*. This is a study of changes in popular sayings like proverbs and riddles in the second half of the 20th century.

The phrase *blason populaire* was apparently coined by a French scholar in the mid 19th century to describe traditional expressions of local identity and rivalry. These sayings serve as emblems of how people see their own groups or how they regard rivals. People use these expressions to characterize their own community or to describe other places or groups (usually disparagingly). Thus they convey self-esteem: often by taunting at others. They can be nicknames for the inhabitants of a particular place, as well as phrases describing them or jokes aimed at them.

Phrases boosting one's own community are things like "Britain can take it" (or "London can take it") – popular during the Blitz in the Second World War, or "There's only one..." which is sung in praise of various football teams. Derogatory phrases about others include such sayings as "Life stops north of Watford" and "The only good thing to come out of Chesterfield is the road to Sheffield" (recalling Samuel Johnson's assertion that "The noblest prospect which a Scotsman ever sees, is the high road that leads him to England!"). These latter phrases are fraught with difficulties in today's climate of political correctness, as it is hard to quote anything that insults any group, even if it is used with good humour.

Nevertheless such sayings have been around for centuries: summing up, however crudely or stereotypically, how countries feel about one another. That is why our language is full of phrases including the word "Dutch" – in the words of the OED – "largely due to the rivalry and enmity between the English and Dutch in the 17th century". The OED adds in small print: "Often with allusion to the drinking habits ascribed to the Dutch; also to the broad heavy figures attributed to the Netherlanders, or to their flat-bottomed vessels". These insulting phrases include *Dutch courage* (i.e. courage assisted by alcohol), *in Dutch* (meaning "in trouble"), a *Dutch concert* (an uproar), *Dutch treat* (an ungenerous treat) and *double Dutch*. And we confirm statements by tacking on the phrase "...or I'm a Dutchman". One dictionary even lists *Dutch nightingale* as a phrase for a frog and *Dutch act* as a synonym for suicide.

Yet we manage to dislike most other countries at some time or other, leading to such dismissive terms as *Krauts, Frogs, Chinks, Eyeties, kikes, wops,* and *Taffy* and *Fritz* – which are all now rightly frowned upon. We also talk about *the French disease* (syphilis) and *taking French leave*, and we call condoms *French letters* – although the French apparently retaliate by calling them *redingotes d'Angleterre* (English overcoats) or *capotes Anglaises* (English cloaks). A book on *Passing English of the Victorian Era* records *German gospel* (meaning vain boasting), *Irish draperies* (cobwebs) and *Italian quarrel* (death or treachery).

Other countries get their own back by calling us *Limeys, gringos* or even *goddams*. Daniel Defoe notes that "The English are a swearing nation" is a common assumption in continental Europe. Apparently the French say "To swear like an Englishman", while the Germans say "To swear like a Frenchman". The Italians say "Only Englishmen and dogs walk in the sun" – a slur which Noel Coward recalled in a popular song.

Every nationality seems to have its faults. A Spanish proverb says "The Englishman is a tippler; the Frenchman is a cur; the Dutchman is a peasant".

Many examples of *blason populaire* take this triple form, as in "The Italian is wise before he undertakes a thing; the German when he is doing it; and the Frenchman when it is over".

Auguste Canel's *Blason Populaire de la Normandie* (1859) gave evidence that virtually every region of Normandy boasts about itself and sneers at every other region. And the people of Normandy have stereotypes about themselves, agreeing that Normans have five qualities: "Traître, gourmand, pillard, flatteur et menteur" (traitor, glutton, plunderer, flatterer and liar). *Lean's Collectanea* (1902) lists various sayings which show that name-calling is prevalent even in civilized areas like Oxfordshire, where popular phrases include "Like Banbury tinkers, that in mending one hole make three" and this rhyme:

> Woodstock for bacon, Bladon for beef,
> Handborough for a scurvy knave, and Combe for a thief.

All these examples suggest how one group or nation forms stereotypes about other groups or nations, which can be regarded as harmless fun or as dangerous prejudices that are close to racism. Perhaps we may see how ridiculous they are when we realize that they are extremely widespread: a childish kind of name-calling that many people resort to but which can be dispelled by actually getting to know our rivals better and recognising what we have in common.

10

Names

Nicknames

Blason populaire, with which we ended the previous chapter, basically consists of calling people names.

Spider, pearly, tug, dusty, spud and blanco. What do these words have in common?

They are all nicknames commonly applied to people with particular surnames. Nicknames are sometimes attempts to demean people, but these names can also be applied with no malicious intent.

So, if your surname is Webb, you may soon acquire the nickname "Spider". The other nicknames listed above adhere naturally to people named respectively Gates, Wilson, Miller, Murphy and White.

It may be obvious why people are called Spider Webb and Pearly Gates, but why Spud Murphy and Tug Wilson? Spud goes naturally with Murphy because they are both slang terms for a potato. Tug Wilson has a more debatable origin, although Julian Franklyn's *Dictionary of Nicknames* asserts that Tug is a "distortion of the nickname Chug, which was that of Admiral of the Fleet Sir Anthony Knyvet Wilson".

Such nicknames are so widely used that we may not bother to wonder how they arose – and the origins of some nicknames are buried in the mists of time. The word *nickname* originally meant an additional name. The word started out as *ekename*, meaning an extra name (*eke* is an archaic word for "also"). Then the word acquired an "N" at the beginning: "an ekename" becoming "a nickname" in a mirror-image of the process that changed "a nadder" into "an adder".

Nicknames arise for various reasons. Physical characteristics account for many of them, so that the gangster Al Capone became Scarface, and jazzman Louis Armstrong was nicknamed Satchmo (from his satchel-like mouth).

Even in these politically correct times, fat people still attract the names Fatty and Tubby, which can be affectionate. Iona and Peter Opie reported that schoolchildren use a host of other names for plump people, including Balloon, Buster, Crystal Jellybottom, Falstaff, Fatty Harbuckle (*sic*), Jumbo and Porridge.

One should avoid jumping to conclusions about the reasons for nicknames. I have always assumed that the trumpeter Henry "Red" Allen was so called because he had red hair. So I was surprised to find, in a new biography, Allen's own explanation: "I was light skinned and my face got red when I blew".

Nicknames arise from moral qualities as well as physical characteristics, so that King Richard I was Lionheart although King Ethelred II was the Unready (from an Old English word meaning "badly advised" rather than "unprepared"). The finest jazz musicians are accorded the accolade of names which indicate their high standing: King Oliver, Duke Ellington, Count Basie, Lady Day (Billie Holiday) and Prez (alias Lester Young).

Many leaders or holy men get "the Good" or "the Pious" attached to their first names. Biographical dictionaries list John the Fortunate and John the Great alongside John the Baptist and John the Evangelist. These last two illustrate how nicknames arise from what people do. Many surnames – like Carter, Miller and Smith – probably started as nicknames from people's professions.

Names can become nicknames by shortening, so that Napoleon Bonaparte becomes Boney, Disraeli is Dizzy, and both writer P. G. Wodehouse and cricketer P. F. Warner (who share the first name Pelham) become Plum. Another form of shortening uses initials to represent the whole person, so that US presidents are known as LBJ and JFK, while R. A. Butler is nicknamed Rab.

Nicknames are often disrespectful, with punsters turning Robert Baden-Powell into Bathing Towel and describing Aubrey Beardsley as Awfully Weirdly. Irony is a favourite begetter of nicknames, so that a bald person may be christened Curly and a slow person is known as Lightning.

Nicknames are conferred not only on people but also on things. The *Times* newspaper is The Thunderer; Arsenal football team is the Gunners; Portsmouth becomes Pompey; and Haydn's String Quartet Op.64, No. 5 is called The Lark.

Quiz 9

Can you supply the real names of the people who had these nicknames?
1. *The Maid of Orleans.*
2. *The Widow at Windsor.*
3. *Hotspur.*
4. *Grand Old Man or GOM.*
5. *Billy the Kid.*
6. *The Prince of Humbugs or The Prince of Showmen.*
7. *Prinny.*
8. *The Beast of Bolsover.*
9. *The Incorruptible (or The Sea-Green Incorruptible).*
10. *The Pocket Dictator.*

Pseudonyms

Like nicknames, pseudonyms are alternative names – but they are usually names chosen by the bearer rather than being imposed by somebody else.

"The Wickedest Man in the World" was a name applied to the mystic and author, Aleister Crowley, but he was also notorious for the number of pseudonyms he used for the many books and articles he wrote. One estimate is that he used at least 150 pen-names, including Mrs Bloomer Greymare, Lemuel S. Innocent, A Gentleman of the University of Cambridge, Comte de Fenix, Ethel Ramsay, Lord Boleskine, Mahatma Guru Sri Paramahansa Shivaji, Hilda Norfolk and Percy Flage.

In fact his most familiar name – Aleister Crowley – was partly a pseudonym, since he had been christened Edward Alexander Crowley and was nicknamed Aleck by his mother, which he didn't like. He chose his new name because he had read somewhere that "the most favourable name for becoming famous was one consisting of a dactyl followed by a spondee…like 'Jeremy Taylor'".

This phenomenon of multiple pseudonyms is not as rare as you might expect, although few people match the excesses of Aleister Crowley. Daniel Defoe was just one of nearly 200 pseudonyms used by Daniel Foe, including Nicholas Boggle and Sir Fopling Tittle-Tattle. Georges Simenon published his first novel in 1921 as G. Sim, and he subsequently used more than 20 different pen-names.

Writers of thrillers and whodunnits seem to enjoy using pseudonyms. The poet C. Day Lewis wrote detective stories under the name of Nicholas Blake; John Creasey used a variety of pseudonyms when writing his crime novels; and Ellery Queen was the pen-name chosen by Manfred B. Lee and Frederic

Dannay when they collaborated on detective stories. Ian Rankin has written as Jack Harvey, and Ruth Rendell is also known as Barbara Vine.

The practice also seems to be widespread among science-fiction writers. Ray Bradbury hid behind at least 16 pseudonyms, including Omega, Doug Rogers and Cecil Claybourne Cunningham. H.P. Lovecraft used such names as Edgar Softly, Henry Paget-Lowe and Humphrey Littlewit, Esq.

Pseudonyms are often used by prolific writers to hide the fact that they are writing lots of books, or when they are writing for different publishers or magazines. Because he writes new books so frequently, Harry Patterson uses the names Jack Higgins, Hugh Marlow, James Graham and Martin Fallon. Thackeray employed a variety of pen-names, including George Savage Fitz-Boodle, Michael Angelo Titmarsh and Charles James Yellowplush.

When Charles Dickens published his first article in 1833, he called himself Boz, which was actually the nickname of his younger brother. According to his sister, H. H. Munro adopted the pen name of Saki from the name of the cup-bearer in *The Rubaiyat of Omar Khayyim*, one of his favourite books.

Pen-names can be used to avoid persecution or censorship, as when François Marie Arouet adopted the name Voltaire so that he could publish pamphlets criticising the authorities and expounding unpopular philosophies. In fact Voltaire is said to have used 173 different pseudonyms. Vladimir Ilyich Ulyanov adopted the name of Lenin when he was involved in revolutionary activities.

In the 19th century, many women concealed their identities with pen-names, because serious writing was thought an unsuitable pastime for the gentle sex. Thus the Brontë sisters – Charlotte, Emily and Anne – published their novels under the names of Currer Bell, Ellis Bell and Acton Bell.

The same motive drove Mary Ann Evans to become George Eliot, and Amandine Dudevant to call herself George Sand. When Louisa M. Alcott (of *Little Women* fame) published her *Hospital Sketches* in 1863, she used the pen-name Tribulation Periwinkle. Even later in the 19th century, the South African writer Olive Schreiner called herself Ralph Iron when she issued her first novel *The Story of an African Farm* in 1883, because her campaigning feminist views were likely to be unpopular.

The writer Winifred Ashton took her pen-name, Clemence Dane, from St Clement Danes church in London. Eric Blair employed a place-name in his pseudonym, George Orwell – constructed from the names of the patron saint of England and a river in Suffolk that he loved.

Actors and entertainers often resort to pseudonyms. To join Equity, the British actors' trade union, you cannot have the same name as someone else in the business. So the British actor James Stewart changed his name to Stewart Granger to avoid confusion with the American star of *It's a Wonderful Life*. And David McDonald couldn't use his real name when he joined Equity, so he became David Tennant, famous as one of the manifestations of Dr Who.

British ballet-dancers used to adopt Russian-sounding names to give the impression that they might have trained with the Bolshoi. Hilda Munnings became Lydia Sokolova; Hilda Boot called herself Hilda Butsova; and Anton Dolin was the pseudonym of Patrick Healey-Kay, who borrowed the name Anton from Anton Chekhov. Diaghilev changed Lilian Alice Marks to Alicia Markova, but he anglicized Gyorgi Balanchivadze to George Balanchine. Margot Fonteyn was originally Margaret Hookham: her adopted surname came from her Brazilian mother's maiden name, Fontes.

When many artistic Europeans emigrated to the USA, they anglicized their names or changed them to more acceptable pseudonyms. Samuel Gelbfisch from Poland was anglicized to Samuel Goldfish by the immigration authorities but evolved into the famous film producer Sam Goldwyn. The Russian-born composer Israel Baline became Irving Berlin; Jacob Gershovitz was translated into George Gershwin; and the French-born singer Alice Joséphine Pons turned into Lily Pons (with a hint of a pun on "lily ponds").

Entertainer Asa Yoelson changed into Al Jolson, and Borge Rosenbaum became Victor Borge. Actor Issur Danielovitch Demsky, the son of Russian-Jewish parents, chose the name Kirk Douglas – Kirk because it sounded "snazzy" and Douglas because he admired Douglas Fairbanks.

The same process occurred on a smaller scale in Britain, with Paul Hamburger becoming the publisher Paul Hamlyn, Louis Winogradsky turning into Lew Grade, and Jan Ludvik Hoch becoming Robert Maxwell.

A lot of musicians alter their names – especially in the world of pop music. Tommy Hicks became Tommy Steele; Reginald Smith became Marty Wilde; Roy Taylor became Vince Eager; and Ron Wycherly became Billy Fury. If you notice some similarities in these names, it is because they were all bestowed on the singers by Larry Parnes, a very successful British agent who seemed determined to give pop performers more sexy or striking names. He was nicknamed "Mr Parnes, Shillings and Pence" because of his reputed meanness towards his artists.

Parnes even wanted to change Joe Brown's name to Elmer Twitch, but Joe resisted. Nonetheless, Parnes was responsible for a slew of pop pseudonyms in the fifties and sixties, including Duffy Power, Lance Fortune,

Vince Eager and Johnny Gentle. Under Larry Parnes's guidance, Lancashire organist Clive Powell became Georgie Fame.

Other agents bestowed pseudonyms on performers. Declan McManus was given the name Elvis Costello after Elvis Presley and Costello, the name used by Declan's father when performing as a singer.

Peter Gammond's *Oxford Companion to Popular Music* (1991) tells how the French singer Edith Giovanna Gassion "was befriended by Louis Leplée, owner of the well-known Cerny's cabaret, who gave her the nickname 'piaf' (Parisian slang for 'sparrow') because of her diminutive size and chirpy appearance".

Many pop stars choose their own pseudonyms. Reg Dwight adopted the name of Elton John from the first names of jazz-rock saxophonist Elton Dean and rock singer Long John Baldry. Terence Nelhams chose Adam Faith from a book of names for children: "Adam" from the boys' section and "Faith" from the girls' lists. Robert Zimmerman became Bob Dylan as a tribute to the Welsh poet Dylan Thomas.

In the 1920s, a music hall entertainer named Vernon Watson found inspiration for his pseudonym Nosmo King from a "No Smoking" sign.

During the First World War, the British royal family changed its name to the House of Windsor, as the Germanic-sounding Saxe-Coburg-Gotha was undoubtedly embarrassing when we were at war with Germany. The name Windsor was also adopted by Barbara Windsor, whose real name was Barbara Anne Deeks. She said "I'm very, very pro-Royal".

Some pseudonyms get chosen very casually. When John Ravenscroft was starting as a disc jockey for Radio London, a typist suggested "Why don't you call him John Peel?"

In the film world, many pseudonyms are created by agents, producers and the like. Roy Fitzgerald was renamed Rock Hudson by a talent scout – from the Rock of Gibraltar and the Hudson River. Norma Jean Baker was turned into Marilyn Monroe by a casting director. Bernard Schwartz was given his pseudonym Tony Curtis by a film producer who said "Schwartz ain't a name to get you into the big time".

Yet other film stars selected pseudonyms for themselves. Arthur Stanley Jefferson was happy with his stage name of Stan Jefferson until he realised it contained 13 letters, when he changed it to Stan Laurel. William Claude Dukinfield became W. C. Fields but also used a host of pseudonyms including Otis Criblecoblis, Mahatma Kane Jeeves and Egbert Souse.

If you see the name Alan Smithee in the credits for a film, it is a pseudonym used by directors and others who do not wish to be associated with a film that they worked on. The name David Agnew in the credits for British TV programmes in the 1970s was a similar pseudonym, while Walter Plinge is used in the theatre to disguise an actor who wants to remain anonymous. There was reportedly a real Walter Plinge, a London pub owner.

Real names

Some entertainers have adopted pseudonyms because their real names sounded demeaning or even embarrassing. This happened with Jeannie Carson (real name Jean Shufflebottom), Diana Dors (Diana Fluck), Joanne Dru (Joanna La Cock), and Lois Maxwell (Lois Hooker). John Wayne was undoubtedly glad to have his screen name, as his real name – Marion Morrison – was scarcely suitable for a hero of Western films. Another movie cowboy, Roy Rogers, understandably changed his name from Leonard Slye.

Celebrities have a tendency to saddle their children with embarrassing names. The most famous examples are probably the offspring of Bob Geldof and Paula Yates (Fifi Trixibelle, Peaches Honeyblossom and Pixie), and Mr and Mrs Beckham (Brooklyn, Romeo and Cruz). Rock star Frank Zappa called his children Moon Unit, Dweezil, Ahmet Rodan and Diva, but when Moon Unit had a daughter, the poor thing was named Mathilda Plum.

Pop star Madonna christened her children Lourdes and Rocco, while singer Bono called his son Elijah Bob Patricius Guggi Q – all the names he liked! Gwyneth Paltrow and Chris Martin christened their daughter Apple Blythe Alison, and *EastEnders*' actress Jessie Wallace named her daughter Tallulah Lilac.

In former times, the Puritans christened their children with long-winded Christian names which today sound very strange. This produced people called The Gift-of-God Stringer, Joy-from-above Brown, God-reward Smart, Kill-sin Pimple and Fight-the-good-fight-of-faith White. When a young woman was asked her baptismal name, she replied: "Through-much-tribulation-we-enter-the-kingdom-of-Heaven, but for short they call me 'Tribby'."

Parents are not always aware of the derivations of particular names. For example, when the statuesque American singer Paul Robeson was so named by his parents, they probably didn't realise that Paul means small. The lively American actress Dolores Del Rio may not have known that her first name means sorrows. Beware of unwanted associations when you name your child Rachel (which means "ewe"), Barbara (strange or foreign), Claude (lame),

Hilda (battle), or Ichabod (inglorious). And if you don't want your child to be compared to a bear, avoid the names Bernard (= strong bear), Ursula (= she-bear) and Orson (= bear-cub).

Pet names

People adopt pseudonyms for a variety of reasons, and their motives can be equally varied when they choose names for their pets, and even for inanimate objects.

My first pet was a cat named Twinkle. It got its name from a variety show which regularly used to visit my home town. There is an amazing diversity of names given to pet cats, although they are often christened with conventional names like Ginger and Tigger. Some years ago, a survey of the most popular cat names included Sooty, Smokie, Brandy, Fluffy, Tiger, Tom, Kitty and Blackie.

Yet T. S. Eliot accustomed us to much stranger names in his *Old Possum's Book of Practical Cats* (1939), with such names as Mungojerrie, Rumpelteazer, Bustopher Jones and Mr Mistoffelees. In real life, T. S. Eliot's own cats included Bubbles, Xerxes, Wiscus and George Pushdragon.

It is rather disappointing to find that the poet Matthew Arnold called his cat by the prosaic name of Blacky, although he had another one with the more exotic name Atossa (from the mother of Xerxes), a cat who would sit quietly for hours beside the cage of Arnold's canary Matthias (recalled in Arnold's poem *Poor Matthias*).

Other writers are well-known for their pet cats: Edward Lear for Foss, Horace Walpole for Selma (immortalised in Thomas Gray's *Ode on the Death of a Favourite Cat, Drowned in a Tub of Goldfishes*), and Dr Johnson for Hodge, about whom Boswell wrote: "I never shall forget the indulgence with which he [Johnson] treated Hodge, his cat: for whom he himself used to go out and buy oysters, lest the servants having that trouble should take a dislike to the poor creature. I am, unluckily, one of those who have an antipathy to a cat, so that I am uneasy when in the room with one; and I own, I frequently suffered a good deal from the presence of this same Hodge".

Charles Dickens allegedly had a cat which he called William, until it unexpectedly gave birth to a litter of kittens, whereupon its name became Williamina.

Foreigners also give strange names to cats. In her *Book of the Boudoir* (1829), Lady Morgan describes dining with the Archbishop of Taranto: "He said to me, 'You must pardon my passion for cats, but I never exclude them

from my dining-room, and you will find they make excellent company.'
Between the first and second course the door opened, and several enormously
large and beautiful Angola cats were introduced by the names of Pantalone,
Desdemona, Otello, &c".

You might expect dog names to be different from cat names but a recent
survey showed that Molly is a favoured name for dogs as well as cats.
However, while cat names often refer to the animal's colour or furriness,
many dog names hint at masculinity or nobility – like Max, Sam, Prince and
Oscar – as well as sporty names like Beckham and Tyson. Charles Dickens
had a large mastiff called Turk – although he also had a smaller dog named
Mrs Bouncer.

The most famous dog with literary connections is probably the devoted
pet spaniel of Elizabeth Barrett Browning, named Flush, whose fictional life
was recounted in Virginia Woolf's *Flush: A Biography* (1933). Other famous
literary dogs include Alexander Pope's Bounce and Lord Byron's Boatswain,
who both had poems written about them by their masters.

In more recent times, James Thurber was a well-known dog-lover, whose
pets included the Airedale terrier Muggs, "the dog that bit people". Thurber
wrote: "Mother used to send a box of candy every Christmas to the people the
Airedale bit. The list finally contained 40 or more names".

Naming horses

In the Garden of Eden, Adam seemed to have no trouble thinking of
names for animals. We are told in the book of Genesis that "Adam gave
names to all cattle, and to the fowl of the air, and to every beast of the field".
But it's not always so easy to assign names to creatures. One of the hardest
tasks must be naming a racehorse – a process that can have all kinds of
pitfalls. How do owners pick on names like Arkle, Red Rum or Nijinsky?

There are rigid rules that racehorse owners have to follow when choosing
a name. For example, the Jockey Club specifies that names for foals must
consist of no more than 18 letters, must not use initials (like C.O.D.) or
numerals (except numbers above thirty which are spelt out), trade names,
names of "notorious" people, titles of copyright books, films or plays, or
"names that are suggestive or have a vulgar or obscene meaning".

However, owners or trainers sometimes manage to christen their horses
with suggestive names like Passing Wind and Peony's Envy because the
administrators don't realise that a name is naughty. The trainer Thomas Tate
confessed that he named a horse Haditovski, because "it was during the time

of President Clinton's *faux pas* and we got the name from *Private Eye* who gave Monica Lewinski the nickname Haditovski....I don't think Weatherbys realised that it was rude, so I got away with it".

Weatherbys is the firm commissioned by the British Horseracing Board to administer the naming business. They are guided by the International List of Protected Names which contains more than 4,000 names that cannot be used, generally because they are or have been in use. These include the winners of all the most famous international races: not only the British Derby but also the Deutsches Derby and the Derby Italiano. So you can't use the name Air Express (which won the Queen Elizabeth II Stakes) or Peintre Celebre (which won the Prix de l'Arc de Triomphe). Other prohibited names include Caligula, Call Boy, Cambridge (and Oxford), Gas, Nun Nicer, Old Joe, Omar Khayyam and Wild Man from Borneo. The list also includes names like Norseman and Ujiji, which were somehow accepted by the authorities despite being liable to cause confusion when uttered on the racecourse.

So how do people select names for their racehorses? Some names are obviously chosen because they imply that the horse is a powerful animal, giving us names like Celtic Thunder, Spanish Don, Russian General, Phantom Wind, Native Emperor, and Let the Lion Roar. Others have a touch of ironical humour: Tipsy Mouse, Big Max, My Little Pony, Why The Big Paws, Back At De Front.

Some names play with spelling: Fisio Therapy, Fays Two, Thisthatandtother, Howbaddouwantit. Others allude to the titles of books, films, TV shows, etc.: Brother Cadfael, Colonel Bilko, Harry Potter. Some Newmarket trainers seem obsessed with the TV series *Friends*, borrowing its characters' names like Monica Geller, Phoebe Buffay and Joey Tribbiani, as well as Chandler Bing which is spoonerized into Bandler Ching!

Many racehorses get their names from their dam (i.e. mother). Dinner Time's child was Eight Thirty; Supportive gave birth to Wonderbra; and Eulogy's numerous offspring included Epitaph, Homage, Commendation and Elegy. But the famous horse Seabiscuit (the subject of a book and a film) seems to have been named after his sire (i.e. father), Hard Tack.

Car names

Some years ago, my father gave me a car he didn't want. I didn't like it, because it was bright red and it had a tough-sounding name – Avenger. What kind of car is that for a gentle bloke like me? I pasted the name "Fraidycat" over the "Avenger" badge on the front, but I still felt uncomfortable driving such a brutally-named vehicle.

Have you ever wondered how your car got its name? Do you own a Ford, Vauxhall, Volkswagen , BMW or Renault? If it's a Ford, is it a Fiesta, Focus or Mondeo?

Of course, every schoolchild knows that Ford cars are named after their manufacturer, Henry Ford: the man who supposedly said "History is bunk" (although he actually said "History is more or less bunk"). At least his name has been preserved in history as the name of a car company.

The reason for the names Ford Fiesta and Focus are obvious – respectively conjuring up images of celebration and the centre of attention, But why Mondeo? The brand management company Interbrand claims that the Ford company asked it to choose a suitable name for its new car, and it came up with Mondeo, from Latin *mundus* world.

Vauxhall cars got their name in a more roundabout fashion, originating in a plot of land south of the Thames owned by Fulk le Breant – a 13th-century mercenary employed by King John. The place was known as Fulks Hall: a name gradually corrupted to Foxhall, then Vaux Hall and finally Vauxhall.

In 1857, the Vauxhall Ironworks was set up there and in 1903 turned to manufacturing cars. When the ironworks became too small for this purpose, the factory moved to Luton and was renamed Vauxhall Motors Ltd. Fulk le Breant's heraldic emblem was a griffin, which Vauxhall Ironworks adopted and which is still part of the Vauxhall Motors logo.

Citroën and Volkswagen are two car firms which have something unexpected in common. They both manufactured armaments in wartime.

The Citroën company was founded by André Citroën, who ran a weapons factory for the French in Paris during World War I and started manufacturing cars in 1919. André Citroën's surname originated in Dutch as Citroen – a word for a lemon, which also happens to be a slang term for a dud car!

Volkswagen is German for "people's car". Hitler laid the foundation stone for its factory at Wolfsburg in 1938 but, when World War II began, the factory started making weaponry. When car manufacture was resumed in 1945, the Volkswagen became very popular and was nicknamed "the Beetle" or "the Bug" from its unusual shape.

BMW is also a German company, set up at Munich in Bavaria in 1916. The abbreviation stands for "Bayerische Motoren Werke" (Bavarian Motor Works).

The Japanese firm Toyota got its name from the Japanese city of Toyota, which the company dominates. It appeals to word-gamers because "A Toyota" is a palindrome.

The Italian firm Fiat has a name which is an acronym: it stands for Fabbrica Italiana Automobili Torino (i.e. the Italian Car Factory in Turin).

Mention of acronyms reminds us of the game called Acronyms, where you concoct a humorous or insulting phrase whose words begin with the letters in a name. This is often played with the names of airlines, so that Alitalia becomes "Always late in take-off; always late in arriving" or "All luggage in Turin; aircraft landing in America".

Car names certainly provide a good basis for this game. So a Ford can be described as "Fix or repair daily" or "Forward only; reverse defective"; a Honda as "Had one – never did again"; a BMW as "Big money waster"; and a Chevrolet as "Can hear every valve rattle on long extended trips".

Over in America, the word "Edsel" has become slang for any kind of failure. It was originally the name given to a car manufactured by Ford in the late fifties and named after Henry Ford's only son. For various reasons it was a flop, and the car ceased manufacture within three years.

Other unfortunate US car names include the American Motor Corporation's Gremlin (which the *Concise Oxford Dictionary* defines as "a mischievous sprite regarded as responsible for unexplained mechanical or electrical faults") and Dodge's Demon and Rampage (would you want to drive such devilishly dangerous-sounding cars?).

Yet Japanese motor firms seem to have a similar flair for choosing names that hardly inspire confidence, like Daihatsu's Naked, Mitsubishi's Eclipse Spyder and Delica Space Gear, or Isuzu's Ascender (the last two suggesting that the car may take off into the air).

Manufacturers have to be careful with naming motor vehicles, because the international market makes some choices embarrassing. The Mitsubishi Pajero had to have its name changed to Montero in Spain, because pajero in Spanish means someone who masturbates. The Honda Fitta had to be renamed in Scandinavian countries, because the word has an obscene meaning there.

House names

Some people give pet names to their cars, but more of us give names to our houses. There was a time when *Mon Repos, Chez Nous* and *Dunroamin* were among the most familiar house names in Britain, but these now seem rather old-fashioned as well as hackneyed.

The most popular recent names include such designations as *Rose Cottage, The Cottage, The Barn, The Coach House, The Bungalow, Orchard House, The*

Stables, The Lodge, Woodlands, and *Holly Cottage.* A 2007 survey by Norwich Union suggested that *Dunroamin* is still popular, although outside the top 50. Home-owners devised such variations as *Dun Talkin* and *Dun Struglyn.*

The use of "cottage" in three of these names suggests that people like the idea of living in a traditional country cottage, although it may also reflect the fact that house names are more common in rural areas than in cities.

The popularity of *The Coach House* and *The Stables* reminds us that many houses are named from their original purpose. Other common appellations are *The Old Rectory (*or *Vicarage), The Granary, Mill House* and *The Old Post Office* (you can imagine this last becoming ever more widespread).

Many names describe the house itself (e.g. *White Cottage, The Gables*) or its situation (*Hill House, Woodside, Seaview*), while place-names often crop up – especially places that the owners have visited (*Balmoral, Lark Rise, Braemar, Sorrento*).

Houses don't have to have names, although apparently it is the law that they should all have numbers, and houses are traditionally distinguished by odd numbers on the left of a road and even numbers on the right.

People have given names to houses for many centuries. A temple in Babylon was called *Esagila*, which means "the house that lifts up its head".

Jew's House in Lincoln may be the oldest occupied house in Europe. It was built in 1158 and got its name because it was owned in the 13th century by Belaset of Wallingford, a Jewish woman who was executed in 1287 "for clipping the King's Coin". Jew's House is near Norman House, built between 1170 and 1190.

Of course, stately homes have often been given high-sounding names – like Blenheim Palace, which was named after the Duke of Marlborough's victory in 1704 at a village beside the River Danube, also known as Blindheim. Sir Walter Scott called his house Abbotsford, after the Abbot of Melrose Abbey and the ford across the River Tweed close by. Before Scott extended it, the house was an old farm called "Clarty Hole" – meaning "dirty hole"!

You might expect Somerset House and Exeter House to be in Somerset and Exeter respectively, but they are both in London. Somerset House was built for the Duke of Somerset (who was executed in 1552). Exeter House is the place in London where Bishops of Exeter reside when attending parliament.

One of the most famous houses in fiction is Manderley in Daphne du Maurier's *Rebecca.* This was adapted (perhaps under the influence of Mandalay) from Menabilly, the house inhabited by Daphne in Cornwall.

On a humbler level, my wife's aunt called her bungalow at Lancing *Schwangau* (because she loved Bavaria) but the house had previously been known as *Gwenstan*, because it was owned by a couple called Gwen and Stan. This is actually quite a common way of creating a designation for your home. Sylvia and Ken called their house Sylken, and Alan and Molly used *Alamo*, while Mary and Tony blended their names into *Marony*. But perhaps Renee and Albert shouldn't have called their house *Renal*.

The composer Rachmaninov named his villa in Switzerland "Senar", from the first two letters of his and his wife's first names (Sergei and Natalia) plus the first letter of their surname.

This very personal way of labelling your home is taken to extremes in such facetious names as *Thisledome* (intended to be pronounced "This'll do me"), *Knickers* (in Hemel Hempstead) and *Kwitchurbelyakin* (near Portsmouth). The Clarke family called their house *Clarke Gables*. *Llamedos* looks like a place-name until you read it backwards.

11

Verse and worse

Nonsense

Lots of people write nonsense – but much of it is inadvertent: they write nonsense when they think they are writing sense. Yet some people write nonsense deliberately. One immediately thinks of such writers as Edward Lear and Lewis Carroll. Why do some humans intentionally write nonsense? The impetus to play with words in this way is similar to the reasons why people invent puns, anagrams and other anarchic types of wordplay.

Humans have a delightful capacity for messing about with serious things. Give them some matchsticks and they won't necessarily light a fire: they may choose instead to devise some puzzles or even start building a replica of Tower Bridge. Give them language, which is generally used for serious purposes (communication, education, laws, etc.), and they often play about with it in hundreds of different ways. Writing nonsense arises from the same process of lateral thinking that leads to constructing crossword puzzles, acrostics or riddles.

Paul Jennings wrote that "Nonsense…involves the essential ability to ask *what if?*" Nonsense sees the possibilities in turning things upside down. Yet writing nonsense is not as easy as it looks. DeQuincey said "None but a man of extraordinary talent can write first-rate nonsense". Nonsense is not only irrational – to retain our interest, it should also be amusing or extend our horizons. Too many so-called comedy shows on radio and television depend upon people turning things upside down without the result being funny or revealing. Paradoxically, the best nonsense is not entirely nonsensical; ideally it should open our minds to infinite possibilities.

There are many reasons for writing nonsense. For example, Samuel Foote used it to make fun of a fellow actor, Charles Macklin, who in 1754 gave a series of pompous lectures, open to the general public. At one of these lectures,

Macklin claimed that his memory was so good that he could remember anything that he read just once. Samuel Foote wrote this piece of nonsense and challenged Macklin to remember it: "So she went into the garden to cut a cabbage-leaf, to make an apple-pie; and at the same time a great she-bear, coming up the street, pops its head into the shop, 'What! No soap?' So he died, and she very imprudently married the barber; and there were present the Picaninnies and the Joblilies, and the Garyulies, and the Grand Panjandrum himself, with the little round button at top; and they all fell to playing the game of catch as catch can, till the gunpowder ran out at the heels of their boots".

Of course, nonsense is often composed simply for humorous purposes, as in the monologues of some of Shakespeare's characters, such as Launce in *Two Gentlemen of Verona*, describing his family's sadness at his departure: "My mother weeping, my father wailing, my sister crying, our maid howling, our cat wringing her hands..".

"Beachcomber" (alias J. B. Morton) often used nonsense simply for our amusement, although in this piece it is employed to parody the flowery style of some authors: "I shall never forget that early April morning long ago when Mr Williamson and I went quietly down the swiftly-flowing Doodle in a duck-punt. The stars were still out, and on our left the badges were croaking in the selvedge-bosses. An old heron went caumbling down to Widdenham Furlong. We could see the spindrift of dawn on his rosetted biceps".

Writers like Ivor Cutler have delighted in creating surreal situations from a world of their own, as in this dialogue:

—My leg has gone berserk.
—Goodness gracious what do you mean?
—It's running down the street, kicking people.
—Your leg? Why don't you run after it, and catch it?
—How can I? – How can I run after it and catch it when I've only one leg left? If I hopped along, people would come and help me and I couldn't stand that kind of thing.

Stanley Unwin created his own surreal world by mangling the language (syntax as well as vocabulary), although it sounds sensible if you don't listen too carefully. His book *The Miscillian Manuscript* described the island of Miscily, beginning: "What does one expect from this little island situate on the north-west corm of the Thracian archipeligole? The map marking – footy free in latitude south – is exactly half way and it is usefold to verify this on an ordinant map which is detail right down to the smallest".

Notice how this nonsense is basically sensible writing with changes to only a few words. This leads us on to the subject of nonsense words.

Nonsense words

I have already mentioned such pioneers of nonsense as Edward Lear. Lear's
Book of Nonsense (1845) actually consisted entirely of limericks, like this one:

> There was an old man of the Isles,
>
> Whose face was pervaded with smiles;
>
> He sang "High dum diddle",
>
> And played on the fiddlle,
>
> That amiable old man of the Isles.

The use of "high dum diddle" reminds us of the nonsensical words that
help to fill out so many nursery rhymes and folk songs. We often encounter
the phenomenon in Shakespeare's songs, such as:

> It was lover and his lass,
>
> With a hey, and a ho, and a hey nonino,
>
> That o'er the green cornfield did pass
>
> In the spring time, the pretty ring time,
>
> When birds do sing, hey ding-a-ding, ding,
>
> Sweet lovers love the spring.

More recent examples of songs with nonsensical words include *Ta-ra-ra
Boom-dee-ay* (originating in 1891 as *Ta-ra-ra-bom-der-e*), Lionel Hampton's jazz
classic *Hey-Ba-Ba-Re-Bop* (1946), Little Richard's 1957 hit *Tutti Frutti*
("Awopbopaloobopawopbamboom") and the following year's Don Lang hit
Witch Doctor ("Ooh-ee, ooh-ah-ah, Bing-bang, wallah-wallah-bing-bang").
The Viscounts had a hit in 1961 with *Who Put the Bomp (in the Bomp-a-Bomp-
a-Bomp)?* Such "novelty songs" were anticipated in 1943 by *Mairzy Doats*,
which told us that "Mairzy doats and dozy doats and little lambsitivey".

The eccentric jazzman Slim Gaillard created a whole nonsense language
which he called "Vout" and employed in such songs as *Vout Oreenee* and *Vol
Vistu Gaily Star*. Much of Gaillard's gibberish made new words by simply
adding such suffixes as "-oroonie" and "-voutie". In his book *On the Road*,
Jack Kerouac said "To Slim Gaillard the whole world was just one big
'oroonie'". Slim Gaillard's most famous song is *Cement Mixer*, in which
virtually the only lyric is "Cement mixer, puttee puttee". But jazz performers
are well-known for devising meaningless words to use in scat singing:
wordless vocals which may have been first used by Louis Armstrong when he
forgot the words of a particular song.

Edward Lear's poems contain plenty of nonsensical coinages, including
borascible, flumpetty, meloobious, mumbian, scroobious and slobaciously, as
well as the one in the last line of :

There was a young person of Crete,
Whose toilet was far from complete;
She dressed in a sack
Spickle-speckled with black
That ombliferous person of Crete.

The *locus classicus* for nonsense words is Lewis Carroll's poem *Jabberwocky* (from *Through the Looking-Glass*) which begins:

'Twas brillig, and the slithy toves
Did gyre and gimble in the wabe:
All mimsy were the borogoves,
And the mome raths outgrabe.

Several words from this poem have actually been accepted into standard English. For example, the word *mimsy* can be found in the *Concise Oxford Dictionary,* defined as "rather feeble and prim or over-restrained" and explained as a blend of *miserable* and *flimsy*. *Jabberwocky* has also given us such respectable words as *chortle* and *galumph*, which are both blends (probably *chuckle* plus *snort*, and *gallop* plus *triumph*).

The dangerous animals invented by Lewis Carroll – like the jubjub bird and the frumious bandersnatch – remind us that nonsense writers love to devise imaginary creatures with strange-sounding names. Edward Lear created not only the Jumblies but also the Pobble Who Has No Toes and the Yonghy-Bonghy-Bo. A similar creature with very strange habits is the oozlum bird, defined in the OED as "a mythical or unrecognized bird" but described more precisely on its first occurrence in W. T. Goodge's *Hits, Skits and Jingles* (1899):

It's a curious bird, the oozlum,
And a bird that's mighty wise,
For it always flies tail-first to
Keep the dust out of its eyes!

Thomas Hood the younger (1935-74) wrote a "Quadrupedremian Song" which starts like this:

He dreamt that he saw the Buffalant,
And the spottified Dromedaraffe,
The blue Camelotamus, lean and gaunt,
And the wild Tigeroceros calf.

Writers also like to invent outrageous names for human beings, as in Henry Carey's *Tragedy of Chrononhotonthologos* (1734), which includes such characters as Aldiborontiphoscophornio and Fadladinida, Queen of Queerumania. W. S. Gilbert (of Gilbert & Sullivan fame) wrote *The Bab*

Ballads, which contain poems with titles like "The Baron Klopfzetterheim" and "Sir Barnaby Bampton Boo".

Limericks

Perhaps the commonest form of playful verse is the limerick.

Limerick is a town and county in the south-west of Ireland, and nobody quite knows how it gave its name to a poem of five lines with a particular galloping rhythm (known technically as anapaestic). Jean Harrowven's *The Limerick Makers* claims to have found the origin in an 18th-century group of poets in the village of Croom in County Limerick who delighted in creating five-line verses in the style which later became known as limericks.

The OED says *limerick* came from convivial parties where nonsense songs were extemporized and interspersed with the refrain "Will you come up to Limerick?" The OED's earliest example is from 1896, in a letter by Aubrey Beardsley, although the word is also found in Rudyard Kipling's *Stalky & Co* (1899) which is based on Kipling's experiences at the United Services College between 1878 and 1882.

The verse-form is actually found much earlier – for example, in a 14th-century manuscript which contains this poem:

> The lion is wonderly strong
> And full of the wiles of woe;
> And whether he play,
> Or take his prey,
> He cannot do but to slo (i.e. slay).

Certainly some Shakespeare songs – like Iago's drinking-song in *Othello* or Ophelia's mad song in *Hamlet* – have roughly the same structure as the limerick, although they are not comic poems.

Coleridge's *Rime of the Ancient Mariner* also has a structure which makes some verses sound like limericks:

> "God save thee, ancient mariner!
> From the friends that plague thee thus!
> Why look'st thou so?"
> "With my cross-bow
> I shot the albatross".

The first collection of genuine limericks seems to have been published in 1820. In their *Nursery Companion,* Iona and Peter Opie quote from this book, *The History of Sixteen Wonderful Old Women.* One of the 16 verses alludes to a lottery which was as popular in 1820 as it is today:

There was an old woman of Ealing,
She jumped till her head touched the ceiling,
When 2 1 6 4
Was announced at her door,
As a prize to the old woman of Ealing.

This limerick takes the form adopted by the most famous exponent of limericks: Edward Lear. In most of his limericks, the last line is roughly the same as the first line:

There was a young lady of Greenwich,
Whose garments were border'd with spinach;
But a large spotty calf
Bit her shawl quite in half,
Which alarmed that young lady of Greenwich.

Many people imagine that Lear invented the limerick but his first *Book of Nonsense* was not published until 1846. Lear claimed he was inspired to write limericks by "the sick man of Tobago", a poem which is mentioned in the second chapter of Charles Dickens's *Our Mutual Friend*:

There was a sick man of Tobago
Lived long on rice-gruel and sago;
But at last, to his bliss,
The Physician said this:
"To a roast leg of mutton you may go".

The Tobago limerick was first published in 1821 or 1822. It illustrates the tendency to include a tortuous piece of wordplay in the last line – or at least a surprising punch-line. This pattern was followed in limericks written by Lewis Carroll:

There was a young man of Oporta,
Who daily got shorter and shorter.
The reason, he said,
Was the hod on his head,
Which was filled with the heaviest mortar.

Ronald Knox, another writer with Oxford connections, composed a famous limerick about Berkeley's idea that things only exist when they are perceived:

There once was a man who said, "God
Must think it exceedingly odd
If he finds that this tree
Continues to be
When there's no one about in the Quad".

A wit replied as follows:

> Dear Sir, your astonishment's odd;
>
> I am always about in the Quad;
>
> And that's why this tree
>
> Continues to be,
>
> Since observed by, Yours faithfully, God.

Some limericks are so familiar as to become quotations, such as the following which is included in the *Oxford Dictionary of Modern Quotations:*

> There was a faith-healer of Deal
>
> Who said, "Although pain isn't real,
>
> If I sit on a pin
>
> And it punctures my skin,
>
> I dislike what I fancy I feel".

The same dictionary includes this famous limerick, written by Dixon Lanier Merritt in 1913:

> Oh, a wondrous bird is the pelican!
>
> His beak holds more than his belican.
>
> He takes in his beak
>
> Food enough for a week,
>
> But I'll be damned if I know how the helican.

Many famous authors have tried their hands at this apparently trivial form of poetry. These include Mark Twain, who wrote the following (in which "Co". has to be pronounced as "Company"):

> A man hired by John Smith & Co.
>
> Loudly declared he would tho.
>
> Man that he saw
>
> Dumping dirt near his store.
>
> The drivers, therefore, didn't do.

W. S. Gilbert wrote many verses in limerick form for the operettas he composed with Arthur Sullivan. In *Patience*, he makes Bunthorne sing:

> I shall, with cultured taste,
>
> Distinguish gems from paste,
>
> And "High diddle diddle"
>
> Will rank as an idyll
>
> If I pronounce it chaste.

Gilbert also parodied one of Edward Lear's weaker limericks with the following:

> There was an old man of St Bees,
>
> Who was stung in the arm by a wasp.

When asked, "Does it hurt?"

He replied, "No, it doesn't,

I'm so glad it wasn't a hornet".

This may have started the fashion for limericks which confound our expectations with their final line:

There was a young man of Japan

Whose limericks never would scan.

When someone asked why,

He replied with a sigh,

"It's because I always try to get as many words into the last line as I
    possibly can".

As a follow-up, Martin Gardner supplied this:

Another young poet in China

Had a feeling for rhythm much finer.

His limericks tend

To come to an end

Suddenly.

Gardner himself capped this with:

There was a young lady of Crewe

Whose limericks stopped at line two.

Limericks can be used in a game, often played on the BBC Radio 4 programme *I'm Sorry I Haven't a Clue*, where the contestants are given the first line and have to improvise the remaining four lines in turn. Limerick contests became a craze during 1907 and 1908 (and again in 1930), with prizes offered to the person who completed a limerick most inventively.

Magazines and newspapers ran limerick competitions, in which the first four lines of a limerick were given and readers were challenged to supply the fifth line.

Advertisers caught on to the appeal of these competitions, and challenged people to come up with the last line of a limerick "plugging" an advertised product. These contests probably became a craze because huge prizes were offered to winners – such as a freehold house or an income for life. The popularity of the competitions was underlined in 1908, when the Postmaster-General told Parliament that sales of sixpenny postal orders (the usual fee for entering limerick contests) had risen from less than a million to 11 million.

The craze was reflected in a musical play produced by Seymour Hicks at London's Aldwych Theatre in 1907. It included a song called *Limericks* in which six characters sang a limerick each, including:

There was a young lady of Erskine,
Who had a remarkable fair skin.
I said to her: "Mabel,
You look sweet in your sable".
She said: "I look best in my bear skin".

Even George Bernard Shaw liked limericks, although he noted that many of them were unprintable. The wordplay and surprises in limericks provide excellent opportunities for rudery and *double entendres*. Arnold Bennett said "All I have to say about limericks is that the best ones are entirely unprintable".

Bennett almost proved the point by composing the following limerick, which is certainly capable of misinterpretation:

There was a young plumber of Leigh
Was plumbing a maid by the sea.
Said the maid, "Cease your plumbing,
I think someone's coming".
Said the plumber, still plumbing, "It's me".

Double dactyls

A double dactyl is a word like *higgledy-piggledy* or *jiggery-pokery* which is pronounced with the rhythm of two dactyls, a dactyl being a stressed syllable followed by two unstressed syllables (it gets its name from the Greek word for a finger, which has three joints). This galloping rhythm is familiar from such poems as Robert Browning's "How They Brought the Good News from Ghent to Aix":

I sprang to the stirrup, and Joris, and he;
I galloped, Dirck galloped, we galloped all three.

It is also found in childish verses like A. A. Milne's "Christopher Robin goes hoppity-hoppity".

Double dactyl came to be used as the name for a type of short poem consisting of two stanzas of four lines each, usually being satirical or ironical at someone's expense. This type of verse is also called higgledy-piggledy, jiggery-pokery and niminy-piminy. The first three lines of each stanza are double dactyls, while lines four and eight (which must rhyme) each consist of a dactyl and an extra syllable. The usual structure is that the first line is nonsense, the second line is a proper name, and the fifth, sixth or seventh line is a single double-dactylic word (like gastrointestinal or parthenogenesis). Here is an example which helps to clarify the structure:

Higgledy-piggledy
Dactyls in dimeter,
Verse form with choriambs
(Masculine rhyme).

One sentence (two stanzas)
Hexasyllabically
Challenges poets who
Don't have the time.

This kind of verse was popularized by Anthony Hecht and John Hollander, who in the mid-1960s published a book entitled *Jiggery-Pokery: A Compendium of Double Dactyls*. Double dactyls are a perennial theme for competitions in the *New Statesman*. These have produced entries like the following:

Drivverel-doggerel
William McGonagall,
Ace poetaster and
Champion bard!

Master of bathos and
Irrationality,
Stunning banality—
Glorious card!

Double dactyls seem to encourage a lack of respect for old-fashioned values. Those of a nervous or delicate disposition should look away now:

Misericordia!
College of Cardinals,
Nervously rising to
Whisper its will:

"Rather than being so
Unecumenical,
Can't we just quietly
Swallow the Pill?"

And then there is:

Higgledy piggledy
Oedipus Tyrranos
Murdered his father, used
Mama for sex.

This mad debauch, not so
Incomprehensibly

Left poor Jocasta and
Oedipus wrecks.
Let's close with a more dignified tribute:
Flippity-floppity
Thomas A. Edison
Searched in his brain for a
New kind of spark.

Gathered together some
Paraphernalia,
Then brought the world in from
Out of the dark.

Clerihews

The clerihew was invented by E. C. Bentley, a writer probably best known for his detective novel *Trent's Last Case* . He was an Oxford graduate, having studied at Merton College, where he failed to get the First in Greats he expected – something that rankled for the rest of his life.

The clerihew was named after Bentley himself – as his full name was Edmund Clerihew Bentley. Clerihew was his mother's original surname, which George Black's *The Surnames of Scotland* describes as "an Aberdeenshire surname", noting that "William Clerihew of Kegge was convicted of profanation of the Lord's day, etc., in 1644".

E. C. Bentley's 1906 book *Biography for Beginners* (published as by "E. Clerihew, B.A.") introduced the world to this verse-form. The book was illustrated by G. K. Chesterton, who had been a friend of Bentley's since their days at St Paul's School. Bentley actually wrote his first clerihew at St Paul's when he was only 16 years old:

Sir Humphry Davy
Abominated gravy.
He lived in the odium
Of having discovered sodium.

This set the pattern for the clerihew, which basically has four lines, rhyming *aabb*. The metre is often uneven – sometimes disconcertingly so – and the tone is generally frivolous, often absurd. The first line usually consists of the name of a person who is then portrayed disrespectfully: like a caricature in verse. Bentley's 1906 collection of clerihews opened with this:

The art of biography
Is different from geography.

Geography is about maps,
But biography is about chaps.
Perhaps the most famous clerihew is this:
Sir Christopher Wren
Said, "I am going to dine with some men.
If anybody calls,
Say I am designing St Paul's".
Some of Bentley's clerihews used atrocious puns, like:
Alfred, Lord Tennyson
Lived upon venison;
Not cheap, I fear,
Because venison's deer.
Like double dactyls, clerihews are a favoured subject for competitions in such magazines as the *New Statesman* and the *Spectator*, whose readers have produced examples like this:
That Narcissus
Should acquire a missus
Was an idea that he rejected
After he'd reflected.
E. C. Bentley's son, Nicolas, won a magazine prize with this example:
Mr Cecil B. de Mille,
Sorely against his will,
Was persuaded to leave Moses
Out of the Wars of the Roses.
A competition in the *Sunday Times* produced this clever entry from 11-year-old Tom Smith:
Margaret Thatcher
Sat in the house and tried to hatch a
Plan to win her Cabinet's approval
Before her removal.
Some of the entries in magazine competitions display remarkable ingenuity in their rhymes:
The artificial opulence of Deauville
Makes any normal decent cove ill:
If there's a place more insincere it's
Biarritz.

Though Shoreham
Is a model of decoreham
It's not half so excighton
As Brighton.

The *Spectator* asked readers to supply clerihews in which the rhymes were eye-rhymes. This resulted in the following:

> Auberon Waugh
> Makes some people laugh,
> But fewer, I gather,
> Than his father.

> Debussy
> Was terribly fussy.
> It took him ages
> To compose "Images".

The poet W. H. Auden wrote more than 60 clerihews in his *Academic Graffiti,* including these:

> My first name, *Wystan,*
> Rhymes with *Tristan,*
> But – O dear! – I do hope
> I'm not quite such a dope.

> Henry Adams
> Was mortally afraid of Madams:
> In a disorderly house
> He sat quiet as a mouse.

> Oscar Wilde
> Was greatly beguiled,
> When into the Café Royal walked Bosie
> Wearing a tea-cosy.

12

Letters alone

Vowels and consonants

It is strange how many things we accept without ever questioning them or wondering about their origins. While watching the TV game-show *Countdown*, I was struck by the way that most of us accept "vowels" and "consonants" without knowing why our language is composed of these two kinds of letters. Which came first – vowels or consonants – and how do they differ?

The generally accepted view is that consonants preceded vowels. The North Semitic Alphabet, which was the forerunner of our English alphabet, consisted purely of consonants. The importance of consonants is illustrated by the fact that it is generally easier to understand words without vowels than words without consonants. For instance, if I write: "He bought a C-R", you could probably guess that he bought a car, whereas if I wrote "He bought a -A-", it would be harder to guess if he purchased a car, bat, can, fan, hat, jar, mat, nag, etc. etc. So the consonants might be called the skeleton or bones of words, while the vowels supply the flesh.

The ancient Greeks added vowels to the alphabet, so that today we have five vowels – A, E, I, O and U – even though these are actually used to represent 20 different sounds (although Scottish English only uses the vowels for 14 different sounds). Y can also be included amongst the vowels, as it is often used to sound like the letter I, except at the start of words (like *yard* and *yes*). The letter W has a similar quality – used as a consonant in *win* and *want* but as a vowel in *own* and *cow*. But note that, in Welsh, W normally represents a vowel-sound, leading to words like *cwm* and *crwth* which sound unexceptional even though they look as if they consist entirely of consonants.

Consonants are defined by some dictionaries as letters or sounds in which the breath is obstructed, while vowels are pronounced with no interruption to the breath. Yet this is not universally true: consonants are often not even sounded – like the B in *lamb,* the H in *honest* and the M in *mnemonic.*

Vowels are not always sounded either: for example, the letter E can be used simply to indicate that a preceding vowel is lengthened (as in *mate,* which might be pronounced *mat* without the E).

The phenomenon of unsounded letters can be used in a game I call Telephoneys or Crossed Lines, where you think of words that can deliberately mislead someone when you are spelling out names or words on the telephone.

For instance, if your surname is Page and you want to clarify it for someone you are talking to, you can say "P as in pant, A as in alpha, G as in golf, and E as in echo". However, if you want to be really unhelpful, you could say "P as in phew. A as in aisle, G as in gnaw, and E as in ere".

When I set this as a problem in my book *Oxford Word Challenge,* I managed to supply nearly a full alphabet of these misleading words. The letters F, L, N and R proved difficult but the remainder were: aesthetic, bdellium, cue, djinn, eye, gnosticism, honour, impasse, Janacek, knee, mnemonic, ouija-board, pneumonia, quay, see, Tchaikovsky, urn, Vaterland, why, xylophone, you and zarzuela.

If you wanted a word with a silent L at the beginning, you might use Welsh words that start with a double L, like Llanfair, the Lleyn Peninsula, or Llanfairpwllgwyngyllgogerychwyrndrobwllllantysiliogogogoch, which are all place-names pronounced something like thl- or chl-.

If you allow silent letters in the middle of words, you could solve F, L, N and R by using halfpenny for F and L, damned for N, and forecastle for R.

Hergé's famous *Adventures of Tintin* include a couple of clueless detectives called Thomson & Thompson (Dupond & Dupont in the original French), who were notorious for trying to distinguish themselves from one another by giving misleading clues to their names. Thompson tends to say things like "Thompson with a P, as in psychology (or Philadelphia)". In *The Seven Crystal Balls,* the other one, speaking on the phone, says: "This is Thomson...No, without a P, as in Venezuela".

In fact there is a huge number of English words containing unsounded letters. Many of these occur in common collocations. For example, the G is usually silent when it precedes an N, as in gnash, gnat and gnaw. Flanders & Swann made a comic song out of this phenomenon by deliberately pronouncing the G in "I'm a G-nu".

Similarly the K is usually silent when it is followed by N, as in knee, knife, know and knight. The last two of these words suggest why silent letters can sometimes be useful, because the K in know makes it different from the similarly-pronounced no, and in knight the K distinguishes it from night. At one time the K in knight was sounded, so that the word was pronounced something like k-nicht.

Why are there so many silent letters in English? The main reason is that we speak a mongrel language: a mixture of words from Anglo-Saxon, Greek, Latin, French and many other languages.

For example, because we borrowed the word accommodate directly from Latin, it contains a superfluous C and M. There is a spare letter A in bazaar, because we took the word from Persian.

The silent M at the beginning of mnemonic exists because the word originally came from Greek. Numerous words starting with P were borrowed from Greek (often via Latin), giving us the unsounded initial in pneumonia and psychology. The RH and RRH in rhetoric, rhythm, catarrh and diarrhoea come to us from Latin.

Ptomain actually comes to us from Italian, although it derives ultimately from Greek *ptoma*, which means a corpse.

Spelling did not start to be standardized until the introduction of printing in the 15th century, before which people spelt words as they heard them. Even Shakespeare's name was spelt in many different ways, including Shakspeare, Shagspere and Shaxberd.

As spelling began to be regularized, some smart-alecs inserted unnecessary silent letters such as the GH in delight (which was originally spelt delit in Middle English) and the S in island (spelt iland in Middle English) – both on false analogies with light and isle.

If you are really looking for confusing silent letters, try some English place names – like Towcester, Worcester, Colne and Greenwich. The East Anglian village of Happisburgh is pronounced haze-bruh, while the Scottish town of Milngavie is pronounced mull-guy or mill-guy. Even more potentially confusing are such surnames as Dalziel (as in *Dalziel & Pascoe)*, Pepys, Featherstonehaugh and Colquhoun!

Phonetic alphabet

A popular BBC radio programme during the Second World War was called *Ack-Ack, Beer-Beer*. The title alluded to the fact that the programme was designed for the amusement of servicemen working on Anti-Aircraft and Barrage Balloon duties.

Ack and *beer* had been introduced in the late 19th century as syllables representing the letters A and B in transmitting messages. The War Office's

Signalling Instructions, issued in 1898, said that "The letters T, A, B, M…will be called toc, ak [revised in 1904 to *ack*], beer, emma". Earlier instructions issued in 1891 had proposed that "B, V, D, E, or M, N, etc. may be called Beer, Vay, Do, E, and Emma and N, etc".

This was the start of a "phonetic alphabet", devised to clarify messages in spoken English. Up to this time, there was a danger that spoken messages could be misinterpreted. This is encapsulated in the story of the message "Send reinforcements, we're going to dance" being passed from one soldier to another and ending up as "Send three-and-fourpence, we're going to a dance".

This phenomenon was turned into a word game called Chinese Whispers or Russian Gossip, in which a group of people pass a whispered message round a circle and see how it gets changed.

The use of the phonetic alphabet caught on before the First World War, so that people used "ack emma" to mean a.m. (the morning) and "pip emma" for p.m. (after noon). During that war, "ack emma" also came to be used for an Air Mechanic or Aircraft Mechanic, and "toc emma" for a Trench Mortar. Australian soldiers used "emma-emma-esses" for breaks in work for a smoke or cuppa (from MMS = "Men may smoke").

The use of "toc" for the letter T became well known through the organisation Toc H, an association to promote a fairer society. It got its name from Talbot House (familiarly abbreviated to Toc H), a rest-house and club for soldiers founded by the Revd. "Tubby" Clayton in 1915 at the Belgian town of Poperinghe. The symbol of Toc H was an oil lamp with a small wick, which led to the phrase "as dim as a Toc H lamp" for people who are not particularly bright.

For many years there was much chopping and changing of recommended phonetic alphabets, because it is difficult to agree on words that fulfil the requirements of such an alphabet. The words need to be short and easy to pronounce and remember. They also have to be very different from one another, so that users can readily distinguish between them.

By 1914, the British alphabet seemed to be established as: Alpha, Brother, Charlie, Dover, Eastern, Father, George, Harry, India, Jack, King, London, Mother, November, October, Peter, Queen, Robert, Sugar, Thomas, Uncle, Victoria, Wednesday, Xmas, Yellow, Zebra. However, by the 1920s, it had apparently changed into: Ack, Beer, Charlie, Don, Edward, Freddy, George, Harry, Ink, Johnnie, King, London, Monkey, Nuts, Orange, Pip, Queen, Robert, Sugar, Toc, Uncle, Vic, William, X-ray, Yorker, Zebra.

Discussions about, and changes in, the alphabet continued well into the 1950s. For example, the letter A could be Ace or Apple, Able or Affirm.

However, the International Civil Aviation Organization devised a phonetic alphabet which was adopted for all NATO countries in 1956 and became a virtual standard. It was: Alpha, Bravo, Charlie, Delta, Echo, Foxtrot, Golf, Hotel, India, Juliet, Kilo, Lima, Mike, November, Oscar, Papa, Quebec, Romeo, Sierra, Tango, Uniform, Victor, Whiskey, X-ray, Yankee, Zulu.

Even this gave rise to some problems, as Alpha had to be changed to Alfa in countries where people didn't know that "ph" is pronounced "f". In France, Juliet became "Juliett" in case the French thought that the final "t" was silent.

This alphabet gave rise to such well-known phrases as *Checkpoint Charlie* and *Juliet Bravo*: the former a well-known crossing point in the Berlin Wall; the latter the police call-sign used as the title of a BBC TV drama series in the 1980s.

This sort of phonetic alphabet is different from the International Phonetic Alphabet (IPA), which is used in some dictionaries to indicate pronunciation. The International Phonetic Association was formed in 1886 and started by using a modified form of the alphabets devised by such people as Isaac Pitman (the inventor of shorthand) and Henry Sweet. But the IPA has changed continually, with numerous extra symbols added to distinguish such things as "voiced implosives" and "alveolo-palatal fricatives". The version used in dictionaries is usually simplified!

Keyboard words

As you sit at the keyboard of your computer (or at your typewriter if you still use one), have you ever wondered why the letters are arranged in such a strange order? Typesetters long ago christened it the "Qwerty" keyboard, from the first six letters in the top row. The American printer Christopher Latham Sholes invented the first commercially produced typewriter in the 1870s. He sold the rights to the Remington company, which at that time was mainly involved in manufacturing firearms!

Sholes devised the Qwerty keyboard primarily to prevent the typing bars from clashing with one another. Of course, this is no problem in computers and word processors but they retain the Qwerty layout despite suggestions that it should be changed. In fact the Qwerty keyboard is standard in most countries: from Bolivia to Iceland, from Sweden to Panama. However, Germany, Poland and Switzerland use QWERTZ; Italy favours QZERTY; and France employs either QWERTZ or AZERTY.

Like the person who found the lost chord, wordplay enthusiasts can find their hands wandering idly over the keys. They may wonder what is the longest word you can type on the top row of the keyboard (QWERTYUIOP)

– and be pleasantly surprised to find that one of the longest such words is *typewriter* itself.

Other ten-letter words that you can type on the top row include *perpetuity, proprietor, repertoire* and *repetiteur*, but these are beaten by *rupturewort,* an eleven-letter word for a plant formerly believed to cure hernias. If we allow hyphenated words, you can manage the twelve-letter *pretty-pretty*, which I am surprised not to find in the *Concise Oxford Dictionary* (although it does include the twelve-letter *teeter-totter,* a verb meaning to teeter or a noun meaning a seesaw).

Cynthia Knight has even used the top line of the typewriter to compose a poem about a poet, including these lines:

> You opt to write
>
> Quite proper poetry,
>
> To pour out your pretty repertoire.

You can set yourself the challenge of finding more words that are spelt with only the top row of the keyboard, such as *pert, quip* and *territory*. You can try the same with the keyboard's middle row (ASDFGHJKL) – although I can't do better than five-letter words like *flags, galas, salad* and *shall.* The bottom row (ZXCVBNM) presents even greater problems because it contains no vowels, although you can use the letter Z several times in a row to represent sleep or snoring!

Incidentally, left-handers should make the best touch-typists, as the left hand types 15 letters while the right hand types only eleven. Mind you, the right-hand thumb usually has to deal with the space-bar, so perhaps that equalizes the chances of developing repetitive strain injury in both hands.

Touch-typists may wonder what is the longest word they can type with their left hand – which uses the letters QWERTASDFGZXCVB. *Watercress* has ten letters; *vertebrates* has eleven letters; but they are both topped by *stewardesses* (twelve letters). As for the right hand, one of the longest words you can type with YUIOPHJKLNM is *niminy-piminy* (meaning "affectedly prim or refined"). As the right hand operates the space bar and most of the punctuation keys, it can type whole sentences as fascinating as "You'll look in upon my jumpy polo pony"!

Quiz 10

From the clues, identify these eight words which can be typed on the top row of the keyboard (QWERTYUIOP). The first is a three-letter word; the second is a four-letter word; and so on, up to ten letters.
1. Part of the body. 2. Chaste. 3. A drunkard. 4. Attractive. 5. A dog.
6. A journalist. 7. Pioneering form. 8. A wild cress with pungent leaves.

Acronyms

Talking of strange sequences of letters, what about acronyms? Strictly speaking, an acronym is a word formed from initials – like UNESCO or CAMRA. If the initials are pronounced separately (as in BBC or YMCA), this is an abbreviation or initialism.

In fact we are surrounded by acronyms and abbreviations, many of them puzzling. A letter to the BBC's house magazine quoted an e-mail sent to some staff: "Users currently registered against an incorrect SLA may recieve (*sic*) the CIC before their official AR has been shown the JML process".

I am glad that I have never had to resort to advertisements for "personal contacts", as it would mean having to decipher the strange abbreviations they use. I can understand WLTM (would like to meet) and GSOH (good sense of humour, which most people ask for, or claim to have) but how am I meant to interpret the advertisement from a woman who "seeks n/s male for friendship" or (even more puzzling) the man "looking for a TV for friendship"?

But modern life expects us to come to terms with acronyms and abbreviations. In recent years we have become accustomed to such shortenings as VDU, HTML, NIMBY (not in my back yard), WYSIWYG (what you see is what you get), ASBO, FAQs and GM foods.

Acronyms can also be made from the first few letters of words, so that Oxfam is short for Oxford Committee for Famine Relief, while a wireless operator who says "Wilco" is confirming that he will comply. In his novel *Pnin*, Vladimir Nabokov coined the phrase "motuweth frisas" referring to the days of the week.

Some acronyms are so familiar that we may not realise that they derive from initials. You may have forgotten that *yuppie* is an elaboration of the initials of "young urban professional". We may not remember that a moped gets its name (via Swedish) from being a cycle with motor and pedals. We have all heard of lasers but we may not be aware that the word comes from Light Amplification by Stimulated Emission of Radiation, or that scuba divers use Self-Contained Underwater Breathing Apparatus.

You may have encountered warfarin as the name of a rat poison or you may actually be taking tablets of it to thin your blood. But did you realise that warfarin comes from the initials of Wisconsin Alumni Research Foundation, with -arin tacked on in imitation of the chemical compound coumarin?

Romantics among us may have encountered the letters SWALK on the back of an envelope, meaning that it was sealed with a loving kiss. This has led to less delicate acronymic messages, like NORWICH (Nickers off ready, when I come home) and WINDSOR (When I'm near, darling, strip off regalia).

Some abbreviations are widely misinterpreted. For example, many people think that SOS stands for "Save our souls" (or "Save our ships") but in fact the letters were chosen simply because they were easy to transmit in Morse code.

Acronyms and abbreviations are often used as devices for covert irreverence or disrespect. Thus enemies are described as NBG (no bloody good) or BOFs, and bad planning is labelled as SNAFU (situation normal: all fouled up – although the F also represents another F... word). Other disrespectful abbreviations include FUMTU (fouled up more than usual), KISS (keep it simple, stupid) and BOGSAAT (an American term for the normal method of decision-making: a bunch of guys sitting around a table). Perhaps we should also include here the lunatic policy of preparing for nuclear war, eloquently summed up as MAD (mutual assured destruction).

Quiz 11

All these questions refer to abbreviations or acronyms.
1. Which two letters after a date indicate "in the year of our Lord"?
2. Which two letters can refer to an organisation for motorists or an organisation for people with a drink problem?
3. Which acronym picks the winners from holders of premium bonds?
4. When applied to milk, what does "UHT" mean?
5. Which Scandinavian pop group was named from the first letters of its members' first names?
6. Which two letters represent part of Canada and an important barrister?
7. Why is a jeep suitable for general purposes?
8. What is the full name for the illness AIDS?
9. In World War I, why were people wary of falling foul of Dora?
10. What is the full name of the Australian airline QANTAS?

Palindromes

Some people may not know what a palindrome is, but they will probably recognize the phenomenon if you quote them an example, like "Able was I ere I saw Elba".

Palindromes are words, sentences, etc. which read the same if turned back-to-front. The example I have already quoted suggests that palindromic sentences describe an unreal world where Napoleon laments the sad effects of exile to the island of Elba (although, as it is doubtful if he ever spoke English, this could palindromically be called an *Elba fable*).

Many palindromic sentences inevitably appear stilted, because they are artificial constructions rather than natural sayings. Even in the Garden of Eden, one would probably not start a conversation by saying "Madam, I'm Adam", especially if it meant that Eve would reply crossly: "I'm a Madam, Adam, am I?" If she felt like fibbing, she might say "Adam, I'm Ada" or even "Sir, I'm Iris!" You can't imagine the conversation progressing much further, with Adam restricted to repetitive statements like "Madam, in Eden I'm Adam".

Palindromes get more artificial as you try to lengthen them, as is clear from ever-longer sentences like "Sums are not set as a test on Erasmus" and "Live dirt, up a sidetrack carted, is a putrid evil".

Some palindromes almost dare you to extend them. You can turn "Dennis sinned" into "Dennis and Edna sinned" and then "Dennis Trebor and Edna Robert sinned". Dmitri Borgmann did even better with the orgiastic 263 letters of "Dennis, Nell, Edna, Leon, Nedra, Anita, Rolf, Nora, Alice, Carol, Leo, Jane, Reed, Dena, Dale, Basil, Rae, Penny, Lana, Dave, Denny, Lena, Ida, Bernadette, Ben, Ray, Lila, Nina, Jo, Ira, Mara, Sara, Mario, Jan, Ina, Lily, Arne, Bette, Dan, Reba, Diane, Lynn, Ed, Eva, Dana, Lynne, Pearl, Isabel, Ada, Ned, Dee, Rena, Joel, Lora, Cecil, Aaron, Flora, Tina, Arden, Noel and Ellen sinned".

There are other forms of palindrome, such as word palindromes. More than a hundred English words are palindromes on their own, from two-letter words like *aa* (a kind of lava), via more familiar words like *nun, deed, civic,* and *deified,* to such long words as *Malayalam* (an Indian language from which we get the words *copra* and *teak*) and *Rotavator* which is a proprietary name of a machine for tilling the soil.

Malayalam and *Rotavator* are the only nine-letter palindromes you are likely to find in most dictionaries, although larger dictionaries may include such words as *evitative* and *semitimes.* Palindrome-fanciers claim to have found even longer words, like *resuffuser* and *detartrated* but these are not exactly common in most daily speech. Yet the *OED* includes a 12-letter palindrome from James Joyce's *Ulysses*: *tattarrattat,* representing a knock at the door.

Proper names can be palindromes too, including a surprisingly large number of women's first names, such as Ada, Anna, Ava, Eve, Hannah, Lil and Viv. Can you think of any palindromic first names for men?

Words which make other words when they are reversed are not strictly palindromes: they are usually called reversals or even semordnilaps (a reversal of "palindromes"). There are hundreds of such reversible words, including *repaid, knits, mined* and *stressed*. One of the strangest of these reversals is the name that Dylan Thomas gave to the place where he set his play *Under Milk Wood*: the small Welsh town is called *Llareggub*.

Quiz 12

Try to solve the following clues which lead to palindromic phrases of two words. For instance, the clue "Prevent blemishes" might lead to "Stop spots", and "A shabby Piccadilly Circus statue" would be "Eros eyesore". 1. Stupid fashion. 2. Lacking male offspring. 3. Market for electric buses. 4. Boring poet. 5. The highest point. 6. A wicked oval fruit. 7. A public school memo. 8. Without a cowboy hat. 9. Clean church seating. 10. The result of open-cast mining.

13

Oddities

Contronyms

This chapter is about some of the oddities that arise in the English language.

Many words have multiple senses, but some words seem almost deliberately perverse in having two opposite meanings. Such words are usually called contronyms, although they are also known as autantonyms, antagonyms or even Janus words (from the notoriously two-faced deity of Roman myth).

For example, *cleave* can mean to split apart as well as to knit together, while *quite* can mean moderately as well as completely, and *sanction* can indicate allowing something as well as refusing to countenance it (the latter sense being clear in the Peace Pledge Union's historic pledge: "I renounce war, and will never support or sanction another"). In his *Spoonerisms, Sycophants and Sops* (1988), D. C. Black listed several other contronyms, such as *scan, let, moot, wound up* and *commencement*.

If you *lease* or *rent* a house, are you occupying it or letting someone else occupy it? If you *trip*, have you stumbled or are you walking gracefully? If you *screen* a film, you show it, but if you *screen* a garden shed, you hide it. If the stars are *out*, you can see them, but if lights are *out*, you cannot see them. Does *literally* mean precisely or is it being used merely for emphasis without being literally true (as in "They were literally killing themselves laughing")?

Modern slang has added to the list of contronyms. *Bad* and *wicked* can mean excellent as well as...er...bad, while *cool* is now a term of approval as well as meaning "unenthusiastic".

Phrases, too, can have opposite senses. *First-degree* murder is the most serious kind of slaughter, but *first-degree* burns are the least serious. The opposing senses of *dispense with* were presumably not noticed by the pharmacist who advertised that he "dispensed with accuracy".

Nowadays, if you say you are going to *take care of* somebody, it may suggest that you are going to kill them rather than care for them. The phrase *waste no time* can mean that you are eager to start something, but that was not the intention when someone (was it Disraeli?) wrote: "Thank you for your manuscript. I shall waste no time in reading it". My favourite such phrase is *with respect*, which is often used in conversation or interviews to imply that the speaker has little or no respect for the person addressed!

Words sometimes become contronyms because of different usage in different countries or contexts. In Britain, if you *table* a proposal, you present it for consideration; in the USA, if you *table* a proposal, you postpone discussing it. In normal parlance, a *handicap* is a disadvantage but a golfer's *handicap* can be advantageous by allowing for the golfer's ability.

I'm sure there are lots more of these contronyms in English, not to mention (is that phrase another one?) those sayings that take on the opposite meaning when they are spoken ironically (compare *Who's a clever boy!* when spoken in praise of a toddler and when said to someone who has done something extremely stupid). Such ambiguity may be useful when an actor asks your opinion of his performance and you reply: "I can't tell you how marvellous you were".

Quiz 13

Try to identify these contronyms from the clues given to their opposing meanings.
1. *Supervision; a failure of supervision.*
2. *A ditch; an embankment.*
3. *To be multiplied by; to be divided by.*
4. *To fix or fasten; to remove.*
5. *A failure; a success.*
6. *To seek advice; to give advice.*
7. *To assist; to prevent.*
8. *Pointed; not sharp.*

Unpaired negatives

Most negative words have a corresponding positive word. So *improbable* is balanced by *probable*, and *unreal* is matched by *real*. But how is it possible to be *unruly* but seldom or never *ruly*? Why can people be *nonchalant* but not *chalant*?

These are examples of the phenomenon known as unpaired negatives: negative words which seem to have no corresponding opposite. You may be *gormless* but can you ever have *gorm*? If a *ruthless* person becomes merciful, can he be described as having *ruth*?

In fact many of these apparent unpaired negatives had a corresponding positive at some time. The word *ruthless* dates from the 14th century but the word *ruth* (meaning compassion) is found two centuries earlier. People are sometimes described as *hapless* (unlucky), a word which dates from the 16th century. But earlier than this there really was a word *hap* (meaning fortune, especially good fortune) which clung on in English for several centuries, although it now sounds archaic. *The Oxford English Dictionary* found the word *unkempt* used by Spenser in the 16th century but the word *kempt* existed from the 11th century (it originally meant "combed").

The earliest example of *unwieldy* may be in Chaucer's *Canterbury Tales*, about the year 1386, but he used *wieldy* slightly earlier in his *Troilus & Criseyde* to describe someone as vigorous or agile: "So fresh so young so wieldy seemed he".

Some of these positive forms, which existed earlier than the negatives but seemed to have died out, have been revived – often in a humorous context. The word *couth* (the opposite of *uncouth*) appeared to have passed out of the language but it reappeared in the late 19th century and seems to have established itself in the language again. In 1896, Max Beerbohm praised Walter Pater, referring to "The couth solemnity of his mind".

The OED lists the word *disgruntled* from 1682. You may not have thought there was an equivalent positive *gruntled* but the dictionary gives it as meaning "pleased, satisfied, contented", with its first example from P. G. Wodehouse's *The Code of the Woosters* (1938): "He spoke with a certain what-is-it in his voice, and I could see that, if not actually disgruntled, he was far from being gruntled".

It seems unlikely that there would be a word like *domitable* to provide the antidote to *indomitable* but the OED actually has two examples – from 1677 and 1836. Similarly, the OED has *peccable* from 1604 to 1992, and *shevelled* from 1613 to 1886.

Several people have used the word *ept* as a deliberate antonym for *inept* – and there are even examples of *eptitude* and *eptly*. The word *abled* is a special case. It was used in the 16th and 17th centuries in the sense of capable or thriving, but it then died out until the late 20th century when it was revived to mean able-bodied (to contrast with *disabled*). Politically-correct speakers then began using it in combinations like *differently-abled*, to avoid saying *disabled*, which might have been felt to have negative overtones.

In his book *The Game of Words*, Willard Espy published a poem crammed with what he called "forgotten positives":

I dreamt of a corrigible, nocuous youth,
Gainly, gruntled, and kempt;
A mayed and a sidious fellow, forsooth –
Ordinate, effable, shevelled, ept, couth;
A delible fellow I dreamt.

Espy also pointed out that many words ending in –less have no matching positive word that ends in –ful. He wrote this poem to correct this "intolerable discrimination":

A tailful dog, one leaf-ful spring,
Set out for toothful foraging,
And as he dug in rootful sod,
Paid voiceful tribute to his God.
At which, a feckful, loveful lass,
Whose strapful bodice charmed each pass-
Erby, cried out, "O timeful sound!
O ageful, lifeful, peerful hound!

Espy might have added many other such words, including *countful, gormful* and *voiceful*. However, there are words ending in –ful that have no corresponding word ending in –less (e.g. *awful, bashful, beautiful, deceitful, mournful*).

Collective nouns

From my childhood as an avid reader of comics like the *Beano* and *Knockout*, I remember a joke about a teacher who asks a schoolboy to give her two examples of collective nouns. He replies: "A vacuum cleaner and a dustbin".

Collective nouns are actually nouns that indicate a group of individuals regarded as a unit – and especially a group of particular kinds of animals. In the latter sense, collective nouns often crop up in pub quizzes, where you are likely to be asked what collective noun is used for a group of (say) lions or ants (the usual answers are *pride* and *colony*). Many of these appropriate words are familiar to most of us: we know it's a herd of cows, a swarm of bees, and a string of ponies. Yet some of these collective nouns are very weird: for example, a parliament of owls, a shrewdness of apes, and a murder of crows. Where did these strange terms originate?

In medieval times, it was regarded as the mark of a gentleman that he knew the collective names for animals that were hunted. As Joseph Strutt noted in his *Sports and Pastimes of the People of England* (1801), "There was a peculiar kind of language invented by the sportsmen of the middle ages, which it was necessary for every lover of the chase to be acquainted with. When beasts were together in companies, there was said to be a pride of lions; a leap of leopards; a herd of harts, of bucks, and of all sorts of deer; a bevy of roes; a sloth of bears; a singular of boars;…a clowder of cats, and a kendel of young cats; a shrewdness of apes; and a labour of moles".

The most famous medieval list of these names is in the *Boke of St Alban's* (1486), a treatise on hunting and heraldry by Dame Juliana Berners, who was the prioress of an abbey near St Alban's. Her book contained a list of "The Companys of Beestys and Fowlys" giving more than 150 collective nouns, including a pride of lions, a swarm of bees, a clattering of choughs, a charm of goldfinches, and an exalting of larks. The last of these words has often been quoted as an exaltation of larks, but that occurs in John Lydgate's *The Horse, The Sheep and the Goose* written around 1430.

One oddity about Dame Juliana's list is that nearly half the collective nouns refer not to animals but to humans. Thus Juliana seems to have originated the playful invention of suitable names for groups of people. Among others, she lists a fighting of beggars, a blush of boys, a blast of hunters, a superfluity of nuns and a herd of harlots. The last of these may remind you of an anecdote about four Oxford dons who encounter a group of prostitutes. The dons try to think of a suitable term for the group, suggesting in turn a jam of tarts, a flourish of strumpets, an essay of trollops, and an anthology of pros. Some versions of the story suggest a peal of Jezebels and a smelting of ores.

Other inventions have been popularized by the titles of novels: for example, John Kennedy Toole's *A Confederacy of Dunces* (1980) and Ruth Rendell's *An Unkindness of Ravens* (1985), although the latter title was also used for a novel in 1967 by Thomas B. Reagan (and this usage is actually found in a 15th-century manuscript).

Collective nouns can refer to things rather than animals and people. We are all familiar with such phrases as a peal of bells and a fleet of ships, as well as a chapter of accidents and a tissue of lies.

The term "collective noun" also has a slightly wider sense – for any word that is singular in form but which describes a collection of things regarded as a unit (e.g. *family, jury, orchestra, library, crockery* and *luggage*). Because these are singular words for plural things, people often wonder if they should be used with singular or plural verbs and pronouns ("the team is playing its last match" or "the team are playing their last match"?). In such cases, many pundits recommend singular verbs and pronouns but others allow plurals when the collective term seems to refer to individuals (the team went on their holidays).

Readers may like to devise suitable names for collections of people – especially people they don't like. James Lipton's book *An Exaltation of Larks* (1970) lists such jokey inventions as a flush of plumbers, a wince of dentists, a string of violinists, a mass of priests, a goggle of tourists, and a descent of relatives.

Quiz 14

Try to think of collective nouns suitable for the following categories of people (suggestions are given in the "Answers" section, but there is no "correct" answer: ingenious readers may do much better).
1. Vicars. 2. Lawyers. 3. Vandals. 4. Teenagers. 5. Critics. 6. Cowards. 7. Egoists. 8. Students.

Outlandish words

One of the games which my family most often plays at Christmas is what we call the Dictionary Game, which is better known to some people as Call My Bluff. This involves choosing an outlandish word (usually from a dictionary), for which players write fictitious definitions. The participants are then presented with all the definitions – including the real one – and have to guess which is correct.

This game can exercise the mind as well as promoting great mirth – although our family tends increasingly to choose words which sound rude (doubtless to get a cheap laugh). Even the *Concise Oxford Dictionary* contains such suggestive gems as *arsis* and *burpee,* which actually refer to part of a metrical foot and a kind of squatting movement. And if you are not an expert at athletics or cookery, you may be surprised to learn that a *fartlek* is a system of training and a *pissaladière* is a savoury open tart from Provence.

It is best to assemble your own collection of notable words, as weirdness is in the eye of the beholder: what looks strange to one group may seem unexceptional to another. Our vocabularies can be very different and they often expand accidentally or in ways that we are unaware of. I can't remember where I came across the delightful concept of the *quidnunc* – an inquisitive or gossipy person who goes around saying the equivalent of Latin "quid nunc?" – i.e. "what now?"

My studies of word games introduced me to the concept of the *boustrophedon* – something written alternately from right to left and from left to right. I only came across the word *wickiup* (an American Indian hut) as the title of a jazz tune, and if I hadn't read Sir Thomas Browne, I wouldn't have encountered the *quincunx*, a useful word for a rectangular arrangement of five objects, with one in the middle and four at the corners.

My association with printers meant that I know that a *wayzgoose* is a summer outing or dinner for printing workers. I was aware of the cartoonist Fougasse long before I learnt that his name is derived from a type of land-mine.

Some strange words can be very useful – especially when we see something and cannot think of the appropriate word for it. What do you call those edible silver balls used to decorate cakes? What is the word for the piece of metal covering the end of a shoelace? What on earth would you call that flap that hangs from the back of military caps worn in hot countries? Or the device from which holy water is sprinkled? You are very knowledgeable if you can answer the preceding four questions with the words *dragées, aglet, havelock* and *aspergillum*.

Most of us never wonder if certain things have names at all. Did you realise that *biggin* is the word for the perforated container inside a coffee percolator, while a *worm* is the curly part of a corkscrew? *Papillote* appears to be the paper frill that some chefs place over the end of a cutlet or bone. And the *petasus* is the winged hat worn by Mercury (or Hermes), the messenger of the gods.

If you can't think of the right word for something, you can fall back on the familiar device of referring to it with a vague term. There are plenty of these: not only *thingummy* and *what-d'you-call-it* but also *dingbat, dingus, doodad, gadget, gismo, thingumabob, thingumajig, thingy, whatchamacallit, whatnot, whatsit, what's-his-name, what's-its-name, whosis* and *whosit* – to which list an American might add *hoopendaddy, whangdoodle* and *wingdoodle*.

Famous last words

Henry de Montherlant made some telling observations about what happens to people just before they die. He wrote: "A lot of people, on the verge of death, utter famous last words or stiffen into attitudes, as if the final stiffening in three days' time were not enough; they will have ceased to exist three days hence, yet they still want to arouse admiration and adopt a pose and tell a lie with their last gasp".

Certainly this tendency has led to the large number of "Famous Last Words" which have been uttered over the years. The *Bloomsbury Thematic Dictionary of Quotations* lists many of these, with the warning note that they are "not always the actual last words said, but include remarks made when dying. Many are apocryphal, hence the fact that some people have more than one set of attributed 'last words'". For example, Oscar Wilde's last words may have been "I am dying as I lived – beyond my means" or the wry remark he directed at the peeling wallpaper in his Paris hotel room: "Either that wallpaper goes, or I do". And when King George V was dying, we do not know if his last words were the public-spirited "How's the Empire?" or the more irascible reply to his doctors suggesting he would soon be well enough to visit Bognor: "Bugger Bognor!"

Famous last words vary widely: from the religious to the profane; from the inspiring to the facetious. Some of the best-known words express noble sentiments, like Edith Cavell's "I realise that patriotism is not enough. I must have no hatred or bitterness towards anyone" or Anne Boleyn's courageous "The executioner is, I believe, very expert; and my neck is very slender".

Executions seem to bring out the best in some victims, as when Sir Thomas More exhorted the executioner: "Pluck up thy spirits, man, and be not afraid to do thine office; my neck is very short; take heed therefore thou strike not awry, for saving of thine honesty". When the executioner asked Sir Walter Ralegh which way he wished to lay his head, Ralegh replied: "So the heart be right, it is no matter which way the head lies". Before being burned at the stake in Oxford, Hugh Latimer told Nicholas Ridley: "We shall this day light such a candle by God's grace in England, as (I trust) shall never be put out".

By contrast, some people's last words suggest panic rather than equanimity. Spike Milligan once said that his father's last word was "Aaaargh...!" Aubrey Beardsley told his friends: "I am imploring you – burn all the indecent poems and drawings". The singer Caruso is said to have departed with the cry "I can't get my breath!"

Others seem bewildered by the process of dying. Nancy Astor asked her son: "Jackie, is it my birthday or am I dying?" to which he replied: "A bit of both, Mum". And O. Henry, the American writer, said: "Turn up the lights, I don't want to go home in the dark".

Perhaps the bravest people are those who laugh in the face of death, making a joke of their final words. When his wife told him that he had accidentally drunk some ink, Sidney Smith shouted: "Bring me all the blotting paper there is in the house!" The American writer Alexander Woolcott told a well-meaning hospital visitor: "I have no need of your God damned sympathy. I only wish to be entertained by some of your grosser reminiscences". And the Irish playwright Brendan Behan is reported to have said to the nun who was nursing him: "Thank you, sister. May you be the mother of a bishop!"

Quiz 15

Who (reportedly) uttered these last words?
1. Thy necessity is yet greater than mine.
2. I shall hear in heaven!
3. You're trying to keep me alive as an old curiosity. But I'm done, I'm finished. I'm going to die.
4. A Roman by a Roman vanquished.
5. That was a great game of golf, fellers.
6. Well, I have had a happy life.
7. Get my "Swan" costume ready.
8. All my possessions for one moment of time.
9. Goodnight my darlings, I'll see you tomorrow.
10. Adieu, mes amis. Je vais à la gloire. (Farewell, my friends. I go to glory.)

14

Answers to quizzes

Quiz 1

1. Antimacassar (it protects furniture from macassar oil).
2. Strudel.
3. Blunderbuss.
4. Fresco.
5. Lacrosse.
6. Vinegar.
7. Trousseau.
8. Chemin de fer.
9. Mafia.
10. Polo.

Quiz 2

1. Bloomers (from Amelia Bloomer).
2. Mach (as in Mach 1, Mach 2).
3. Pullman.
4. Boycott.
5. Bowdlerize (from Thomas Bowdler).
6. Beaufort scale (from Sir Francis Beaufort).
7. Wendy house (J. M. Barrie invented the name "Wendy" for the character in Peter Pan).
8. Mobius (Mobius strip).
9. Biro (from Laszlo Biro, inventor of the ballpoint pen).
10. The Tony award for American theatre.

Quiz 3

1. sauna: 1881.
2. cash dispenser: 1967.

3. mustard gas: 1917.
4. homosexual (adjective): 1892.
5. modern art: 1820.
6. bird watching: 1901.
7. launderette: 1949.
8. videocassette: 1970.
9. escalator: 1900.
10. shorthand typist: 1901.

Quiz 4

(This is just a selection: there may be other possibilities.)
1. The pen is mightier than the sword.
2. It's never too late (or You're never too old) to learn.
3. Too many cooks spoil the broth.
4. Never judge a book by its cover (or Beauty is only skin deep).
5. Fear the Greeks bearing gifts.
6. Birds of a feather flock together.
7. Life is what you make it.
8. It's the thought that counts.
9. Many hands make light work.
10. There's no place like home (or Home is where the heart is).

Quiz 5

Baby grand, dry ice, idiot savant, ill health, inside out, light heavyweight, missing link, pretty ugly, random order, same difference, science fiction, student teacher, sweet nothings, wireless cable.

Quiz 6

(These are only suggestions. You may have been much more ingenious.)
1. Accidental, knocking out your teeth with a hammer.
2. Auctioneer, someone who looks forbidding.
3. Champagne, malingering.
4. Farcical, a long bicycle ride.
5. Fast food, food which makes you think of fasting.
6. Innuendo, an Italian suppository.
7. Life jacket, skin.
8. Maritime, wedding day.
9. Neurosis, fresh flowers.
10. Relief, what trees do in spring.
11. Servile, a very unpleasant knight.
12. Stalemate, your spouse.

Quiz 7

(These are only suggestions.)
1. Wait a Moment by Arthur Mo.
2. Shipwreck by Mandy Boats.
3. The Merry Widow by Gail Adey.
4. Wickedness by Evelyn Tent.
5. Horse riding by Jim Khana.
6. Travelling by Wanda Lust & Sally Forth.
7. My mother-in-law by George Orr.
8. Rossini Operas by Barbara Seville.
9. Mountains of South America by Ann Dees.
10. A Stagnant Pool in Australia by Bill A. Bong.

Quiz 8

1. E. M. Forster's Passage to India.
2. William Golding's Lord of the Flies.
3. Oscar Wilde's Salome.
4. Shakespeare's Midsummer Night's Dream.
5. H. G. Wells's War of the Worlds.

Quiz 9

1. Joan of Arc.
2. Queen Victoria.
3. Sir Henry Percy.
4. William Gladstone.
5. William Bonney.
6. P. T. Barnum.
7. George IV, when he was Prince of Wales.
8. Dennis Skinner MP.
9. Robespierre (French politician).
10. Engelbert Dollfuss (Austrian politician).

Quiz 10

1. Eye.
2. Pure.
3. Toper.
4. Pretty.
5. Terrier.
6. Reporter.
7. Prototype.
8. Pepperwort.

Quiz 11

1. AD (Anno Domini).
2. AA (Automobile Association or Alcoholics Anonymous).
3. ERNIE (Electronic Random Number Indicator – or Indicating – Equipment).
4. Ultra heat treated.
5. ABBA (Agnetha, Bjorn, Benny, Anni-Frid).
6. QC (Quebec and Queen's Counsel).
7. Because it supposedly derives from GP (general purposes).
8. Acquired immune deficiency syndrome.
9. It was the Defence of the Realm Act.
10. Queensland and Northern Territory Aerial Service.

Quiz 12

1. Daft fad.
2. No son.
3. Tram mart.
4. Drab bard.
5. Top spot.
6. Evil olive.
7. Eton note.
8. No stetson.
9. Swept pews.
10. Eroded ore.

Quiz 13

(with examples of the contrasting meanings)
1. Oversight (she had the oversight of the games; forgetting my trousers was a regrettable oversight).
2. Dyke (the dyke filled with water; the boy put his finger in the dyke).
3. By (a six-by-four plank; divide twelve by three).
4. Clip (clip those papers together; I'm clipping his hair).
5. Bomb (his attempt to make money was a bomb; the concert went down a bomb).
6. Consult (consult your doctor; a consulting engineer).
7. Help (please help me; I can't help loving you).
8. Blunt (he made some blunt remarks; a blunt instrument).

Quiz 14

1. *a bray of vicars.*
2. *a case of lawyers.*
3. *a litter of vandals.*
4. *an embarrassment of teenagers.*
5. *a pox of critics.*
6. *a quiver of cowards.*
7. *a mine of egoists.*
8. *a riot of students.*

Quiz 15

1. *Sir Philip Sidney.*
2. *Beethoven.*
3. *George Bernard Shaw.*
4. *Mark Antony.*
5. *Bing Crosby.*
6. *William Hazlitt.*
7. *Anna Pavlova.*
8. *Queen Elizabeth I.*
9. *Noel Coward.*
10. *Isadora Duncan.*